PRESENT-DAY CONVERSIONS

CONVERSIONS

of the new testament kind

PRESENT-DAY CONVERSIONS

of the new testament kind

Whoso is wise, and will observe these
things, even they shall understand
the lovingkindness of the LORD
PSALM 107:43

FROM THE MINISTRY OF

JOHN METCALFE

THE PUBLISHING TRUST
Church Road, Tylers Green, Penn, Buckinghamshire.

Printed and Published by
John Metcalfe Publishing Trust
Church Road, Tylers Green
Penn, Buckinghamshire

—

First Published 1991

—

ISBN 1 870039 31 9

—

Price £2.25

—

CONTENTS

HYMN 5

Acts 4:10-13

Ellacombe

1 TO you, and Isr'el all, be known
   the truth which we proclaim:
by Jesus Christ of Nazareth,
   and by his holy name,

2 Whom ye did crucify, whom God
   raised up with mighty hand,
by him it is that this man here
   before you whole doth stand.

3 This is the stone which ye that build
   in scorn aside have laid,
but which is chosen, and is now
   head of the corner made.

4 Salvation in none other is:
   'neath heaven verily
there is none other name 'mong men
   whereby we saved must be.

5 Now when of Peter and of John
   the boldness they did see,
and men unlearn'd and ignorant
   perceiving them to be:

6 They marvelled, and took knowledge that
   they had with Jesus been,
and could say nothing 'gainst the things
   by all the people seen.

From THE HYMNS
OF THE NEW TESTAMENT

John Metcalfe

PRESENT-DAY CONVERSIONS

OF THE NEW TESTAMENT KIND

'For the testimony of Jesus is the spirit of prophecy.'

Revelation 19:10.

THE apostles of Jesus Christ, and ministers of the gospel, were required to declare with the voice, and set forth by the hand, the reality of their own conversion.

They were to show their calling to the ministry, how they were gifted, prepared, and sent forth to the work.

Moreover they were obliged to manifest their fruitfulness in preaching and teaching, in the conversion of sinners, the perfecting of the saints, and the edifying of the body of Christ.

Mere words, bare claims, exaggerated statistics, that which might be copied by man, none of these things would do: they must show forth their own experience, their having received the revelation of the mystery, their having been taught from above, their experimental entrance into the divine realities of salvation, the power that rested upon them, the effectual working of the Holy Ghost through them, and the heavenly consequences that attended their ministry.

And this is only right and just before all the people. It is for the ministers of Christ honestly and soberly to justify their conversion and their fruitfulness by showing the signs following, giving glory to God, as did the apostles, and, indeed, as did the Lord Jesus in his being sent. But this is what no unconverted minister, no pretender to what he has not received, no self-sent usurper, can ever do.

Hence, over against such false shepherds, hirelings, and letter-learned actors—some of whom might well deceive the very elect without this simple test—the true minister must stand out: By their fruits ye shall know them.

But unconverted ministers, those who have no fruit, who are not sent, try to wriggle out of their predicament by denying this test. That is why, with affected mock modesty, they claim it to be proud and boasting to do what in fact Jesus and the apostles did by way of example, and what God commands them to do by way of precept.

The openly showing one's conversion, and how God wrought it—not man; not oneself—together with the plain manifestation of one's heavenly and divine call to the ministry, and the spiritual gifts supernaturally given, with all the undeniable proof of conversions and gathering which follow: these things are essential, and to be shown them demonstrably is the right of the people.

Especially is such open, honest dealing necessary in view of the abiding truth that every called minister of Jesus Christ will be subject to the most outrageous slanders, persecutions, evil speakings, and, indeed, will find themselves reviled even as was their Master.

But both the Master and those whom he sends can show the work of God in themselves, on themselves, and from themselves, by the undeniable evidence of their fruitfulness. Whereas all the slanderers, persecutors, and all who speak evil—and write evil—who oppose them, can show nothing at all. By their fruits ye shall know them.

Then, it is right for those called of God to show forth their fruit, just as it is right that those twice dead, without fruit, and plucked up by the roots, should be made manifest in their barren shame and disgraceful practice before all men.

Consider how the Lord Jesus set this example. Observe how he showed and commended his ministry and its divine origin —as that of his Person sent from the Father—in the clearest, boldest manner possible.

Then notice how the scriptural scribes, the fundamentalist Pharisees, the reformed schoolmen, the modernist Sadducees, the worldly Herodians, the hierarchical priests, the traditionalist elders, and the letterish lawyers, all agreed in one to slander, libel, falsely accuse, revile, persecute, and ensnare the Saviour in his ministry.

Hence it is clear, absolutely clear, that they were of their father the devil, for all their outward religion. And the works of their father they would do.

What works are these? Lies, false accusations, hatred, attempts to ensnare and entrap with words, schemes to destroy— at least the reputation of—the righteous, and to besmirch the innocent. And these same things those who are of their spirit do to those who are in the Spirit of Christ to this very day.

Take a few passages showing the holy boldness of Jesus, and the consequences from the religious:

'I that speak unto thee am he.' He said that God was his Father, making himself equal with God. 'But', said he, 'I receive not honour from men.' All men, continued Jesus, should honour the Son even as they honour the Father. 'For I came down from heaven, not to do mine own will, but the will of him that sent me.' 'I am the bread of life.'

The Jews murmured because he said, 'I am the bread which came down from heaven.' They strove among themselves, saying, 'How can this man give us his flesh to eat?' Many therefore of his disciples, when they heard these things, said, 'This is an hard saying; who can hear it?' For neither did his brethren believe in him.

Said he, 'The world cannot hate you; but me it hateth, because I testify of it, that the works thereof are evil.' And, 'My doctrine is not mine, but his that sent me.' There was much murmuring among the people concerning him: for some said, 'He is a good man': others said, 'Nay; but he deceiveth the people.'

'Behold a gluttonous man, and a winebibber.' 'He doeth these things by Beelzebub, the prince of the devils.' 'He cometh eating and drinking.' 'We know that this man is a sinner.' 'He hath an unclean spirit.' 'He hath a devil, and is mad; why hear ye him?'

They sought to trap him. They sought to kill him. 'Is this not he, whom they seek to kill?' 'We know this man whence he is: but when Christ cometh, no man knoweth whence he is.'

And there was a division among the people because of him.

He bare record of himself, saying, 'I am the light of the world: he that followeth me shall not walk in darkness, but shall have the light of life.' The Pharisees then said unto him, 'Thou bearest record of thyself; thy record is not true.'

But his record was true; his judgment was just. 'My judgment is just; because I seek not mine own will, but the will of the Father which hath sent me.' 'If I judge, my judgment is true: for I know whence I came, and whither I go.'

The Jews said unto him, 'Say we not well that thou art a Samaritan, and hast a devil?' Jesus answered, 'I have not a devil; but I honour my Father, and ye do dishonour me.' Then took they up stones to cast at him.

He said, 'I am the door'; 'I am the good shepherd'; 'I am the vine'; 'I am the resurrection, and the life.' 'I and my Father are one.' Then the Jews took up stones again to stone him.

And Jesus said, 'He that believeth on me, believeth not on me, but on him that sent me.' And they all condemned him to be guilty of death.

Neither should the disciple be surprised that he is not above his Master, and that he is called upon to show the work of God in Christ upon his soul, and in his ministry, with similar effect from those whose religion stands in the dead letter and in false charity.

Secondly, as an instance of one sent by the Son of God from heaven, take notice of the ministry of the apostle Paul, who sees to it that his conversion is recorded no less than three times over in the Book of Acts, quite apart from such instances as his testimony in the epistle to the Galatians.

Paul commended both his ministry and his manner of life to his brethren, and not least because of those who went everywhere with false stories at great pains to demean the one and slander the other.

But he spoke of himself on this wise: 'Paul, a servant of Jesus Christ, called an apostle, separated unto the gospel of God.' 'Paul, an apostle of Jesus Christ by the commandment of God our Saviour, and Lord Jesus Christ, which is our hope.' He was sent 'according to the commandment of the everlasting God' for 'obedience to the faith among all nations.'

He asserted that grace was given unto him that he should be the minister of Jesus Christ to the Gentiles, ministering the gospel of God, that the offering up of the Gentiles might be acceptable, being sanctified by the Holy Ghost. He received of the Lord that which he delivered unto the assembly. 'For', saith he, 'the gospel which was preached of me is not after man, neither was I taught it, but by the revelation of Jesus Christ.'

By revelation the mystery was made known unto him, even the mystery of the gospel, whereof he was made a minister according to the gift of the grace of God which was given unto him by the effectual working of God's power.

And who else can say such things? Every called minister of Jesus Christ unto this day can say such things.

And who can never say such things? Every hireling, every letter-learned man-made pretender, every belittler of the true ministry, every persecutor, every poison pen letter writer, every backbiter, every accuser of the brethren: all these can never say such things world without end. All they can do is invent abuse by which they revile and falsely accuse the true ministers of Jesus Christ.

Hence the necessity laid upon God's servants to show the divine origins of their conversion, call, experimental ministry, and abiding fruit before all the people.

Thus the ministers of God may—and must—say, 'In all things approving ourselves as the ministers of God, in much patience, in afflictions, in necessities, in distresses, in stripes, in imprisonments, in tumults, in labours, in watchings, in fastings; by pureness, by knowledge, by longsuffering, by kindness, by the Holy Ghost, by love unfeigned, by the word of truth, by the power of God, by the armour of righteousness on the right hand and on the left, by honour and dishonour, by evil report and good report; as deceivers, and yet true; as unknown, and yet well known; as dying, and, behold, we live; as chastened, and not killed; as sorrowful, yet always rejoicing; as poor, yet making many rich; as having nothing, and yet possessing all things.'

For Paul's rejoicing, the testimony of his conscience, was this: that in simplicity and godly sincerity, not with fleshly wisdom but by the grace of God, he had his conversation in the world, and more abundantly to the brethren.

'Ye are witnesses, and God also, how holily, and justly, and unblameably, we behaved ourselves among you that believe.' Say that today, and one is accused of boasting. Notice, however, that Paul said it then, and was accused of boasting. But he still said it, and by the Holy Ghost he said it. And so do we.

Paul testified that he was an apostle, not of men, neither by man, but by Jesus Christ, and God the Father. Does he begin again to commend himself?

But he would not dare to speak of those things which Christ had not wrought by him, to make the Gentiles obedient by word and deed, through mighty signs and wonders, by the power of the Spirit of God, so that from Jerusalem, and round about unto Illyricum, he had fully preached the gospel of Christ.

'Our boasting', saith he, 'is found a truth.' 'Great is my boldness of speech toward you, yea, great is my glorying of you.' And no man should stop him of this boasting in all the regions of Achaia.

But they would try, day and night they would try. They would try without ceasing, sending their letters, creeping about out of sight behind his back, following him in his work as soon as he had left one place to go to another, slandering, reviling, belittling, despising, and worse.

'We have found this man a pestilent fellow, and a mover of sedition.' 'He is a ringleader of the sect of the Nazarenes.'

Paul was spoken of as an evil doer. He was often put in prison, just as they expected from one of such bad behaviour. Indeed, they felt it their duty to go to the Authorities themselves about this fellow.

As concerning his sect, it was everywhere spoken against.

All this, from those who could give no account of God's work on their soul, who had never been called, who were nothing but clouds without water, carried about of winds.

They were trees whose fruit withereth, without fruit, twice dead, plucked up by the roots. They were raging waves of the sea, foaming out their own shame, for ever filled with malicious envy and jealousy at the fruitfulness of the man against whom they could never, never measure themselves even to the least cubit.

'I suppose I was not a whit behind the very chiefest apostles', cries Paul to their astonishment. 'For I laboured more abundantly than they all.' 'I have therefore whereof I may glory.'

As to the saints, 'Ye became followers of us.' 'Be ye followers of me, even as I also am of Christ.' For 'I am ordained a preacher, and an apostle, a teacher of the Gentiles in faith and verity.' Such words enraged those who so envied him.

They accused him of boasting, of commending himself, of pride. But Paul, and the ministers with him, dare not make themselves of that number, or associate themselves with some that commended themselves. For such, measuring themselves by themselves, and comparing themselves among themselves, were not wise.

'But we will not boast of things without our measure, but according to the measure of the rule which God hath distributed to us, a measure to reach even unto you.' Mark that: not boasting without our measure. And what was outside of Paul's measure? Why, 'other men's labours.' Of these he would not boast, no, not at all. But soberly, justly, and openly Paul declared what God had wrought by him.

He showed the saints his divine calling, his gifts by grace, how God had powerfully inwrought in him both the law and the gospel; he showed his vital experience of salvation; how Christ had taught him in the wilderness; how the Spirit had called him forth; and how fruitful, from that very day, how fruitful were the consequences that resulted from his being sent of God.

And that is the way, as it is the truth, and must be the obligation laid upon every sent minister of Jesus Christ even to this latest hour.

9

And if such ministers can fulfil these conditions, then we know who has sent them, and may safely follow them, and hear their doctrine, giving God the glory, for, 'How shall they preach except they be sent?'

But if those who claim to be ministers, or pastors, cannot fulfil these simple conditions, then we know that God has not sent them, they have sent themselves, and that we are neither to hear them nor to follow them, for we know whence they are, and Christ has strictly warned and admonished us to avoid them—whosoever or whatsoever they may be in the eyes of men—saying unto us, 'Go not after them'.

Nevertheless, he is faithful that promised; indeed, great is his faithfulness—he cannot deny himself—and he will assuredly send us true ministers from his holy presence, anointed, endowed, prepared, and taught by him, full of the Holy Ghost, and seasoned by afflictions, divinely illuminated in the word of God.

Surely these will appear to us in our own day, saying, 'Receive us; we have wronged no man, we have corrupted no man, we have defrauded no man: our mouth is open unto you, our heart is enlarged.'

By the ministry of these, Jesus Christ will be evidently set forth, crucified among us.

We will be constrained to receive them as the angels of God, as Christ Jesus. This is the blessedness of the gospel discovered when preached by such sent ministers.

Where then now is this blessedness of which scripture speaks?

This is a blessedness that shall ever accompany the ministry of the new testament, which is a ministry that neither originates from, nor can it be copied by, the works of man. It is a blessedness which stands in the power of the Holy Ghost from heaven, it is a blessedness that rests on the faith of the gospel, being sealed by the authority of the Son of God in glory.

Of this blessedness the divine fruit which follows such a sent ministry bears witness. And is to bear witness to this day, as it is written 'Ye have not chosen me, but I have chosen you, and ordained you, that ye should go and bring forth fruit, and that your fruit should remain.' Amen and Amen.

The Conversion of Alun Barton

EVANGELISING throughout Great Britain, many hundreds were soundly converted through the ministry of John Metcalfe in the early 1950's. This was very shortly after his own remarkable conversion.

In the winter of 1955 the young evangelist ministered in many parts of Wales, finally preaching at Llandudno towards the end of this period. On the last night, an after-meeting was appointed at the Presbyterian church. This was packed, and a mighty visitation of the Spirit (to the elderly evoking memories of the late revival) was felt by all who were present.

As the hall slowly emptied, John Metcalfe sought out—as he always did—those aged saints who could still remember

11

the Welsh Revival at the turn of the century. One old lady, dressed all in black, had been a young woman at the height of the awakening in 1904. With rapt attention Mr. Metcalfe hung on her every word as the vivid memories came flooding back. When she concluded it was very late, yet, hitherto unnoticed, two men still remained behind, patiently waiting to speak with the evangelist.

The first, Bob Williams, a young man in his early twenties, had been mightily converted in the meeting that night. He was waiting to confess his experience, and give vent to his joy, and could hardly contain himself as he spoke of his new-found Saviour.

The second, an older man, was notorious in the town as an incorrigible drunkard, a blasphemer, a man of evil reputation, foul-mouthed and vile in his behaviour. Yet, for the first time, unwillingly, moved by a strange compulsion, he had been drawn into the meeting that night. He was devastated. The arrows of conviction stuck fast in him, the terrors of death laid hold upon him, and the wrath of God stared him in the face. He felt himself beyond help. There was no hope for him in God. He was an outcast in his own sight. He had gone too far, it was too late.

Nothing that John Metcalfe could say brought the least relief. It was as if Alun Barton, for that was his name, was locked in a cage of despair, and, desperate, believed it impossible that he should ever be delivered. His distress was pitiful to behold. The young evangelist laboured long and hard. But no word, no promise, no entreaty, brought the least spark of hope.

In his own eyes Alun Barton was damned beyond redemption, though convicted past endurance. He had blasphemed once too often, he had blasphemed the Holy Ghost, there was no forgiveness for him. He had railed on the Saviour, he had trampled on the blood of Christ, he was reprobate. Nothing could reach him. No one could help him.

At the point of exhaustion, with nothing left that could be said, empty of words, suddenly John Metcalfe felt a strange, unearthly sensation. He became filled with a profound impression of the heavenly, almost unbearable, compassion of Christ. The sensation was beyond description in its intensity.

Moved past expression, he looked, and looked, and looked again, deep into Alun's eyes, for what seemed like an eternity. Not a word passed. Then the two men clung to one another, their hands gripped, and, still silent, beyond words, they went their separate ways into the night.

Very early in the morning, as the evangelist prepared to depart for his next meetings, there was a knock on the door, and he was called to the phone. It was Alun Barton. He had somehow obtained Mr. Metcalfe's number, and was determined to speak to him before he left Llandudno. This was what he said:

'Last night when we parted I went to my place in despair and bitterness of soul, John Bâch. I lay on the bed, but as soon as I turned out the light an eerie thing happened: I could see your eyes in the dark, as plain as daylight. I was held in the strength of your gaze, just as I was before we parted, those eyes filled with yearning for my soul. I could not stand it. I rose and turned on the light. Nothing. There was nothing to see.

Turning out the light again, immediately the vision of your eyes reappeared, just as they looked into the depths of my soul earlier that night. I felt as if Jesus himself were looking into me: That piercing gaze! It was so vividly real. As if you were in the room. I trembled like a leaf. The presence was so felt, the sight so clear. I rose and turned on the light again. Nothing.

Eventually turning out the light once more, straightaway the vision of your eyes reappeared exactly as they had been, and just as they gazed into my inmost being that evening. The sight was inescapable. Desperately I switched on the light again and waited till I had calmed myself. But as soon as the light was out, the vision reappeared, more palpable than ever before.

This went on all night. Those eyes! Those eyes! I was worn out, shaking and trembling, for there was power, power was present. At the last I could resist no more. I fell on my knees, on my face, and poured out my whole soul to God.

I cried out with all my might. I emptied my very being before the Almighty. I confessed my vile state and evil deeds, weeping my heart out, owning up to all my dreadful sins. The room seemed bathed with light. I felt my burden fall off: I saw the door of hope open: O, praise God, my debts were discharged, my soul was set free: as the filthy leper, I was touched by the hand of Jesus, and immediately I was made clean. To me, it was his very voice I heard: 'Son, thy sins be forgiven thee.'

In the depths of my soul, his eyes shone with pity and compassion upon me, and I knew that I had been forgiven and pardoned, as the love of Christ filled my heart. John, Bâch, I am saved this day, and I knew that I had to phone and tell you before you left Llandudno this morning.'

After this, letters passed between John Metcalfe and Alun Barton, who began witnessing for the Saviour, and singing (for he had a fine voice) in the open air, and throughout the district, a wonderful testimony to saving grace. Eventually, sickened by the deadness of the churches, Alun drifted towards the Open Brethren. John Metcalfe wrote warning him of the danger of a different kind of hardness and dryness, equally dead, though in form apparently more scriptural.

The fervent young evangelist pleaded in his letter for Alun to beware of Arminian easy-believism, false assurance, and specious outward forms. He entreated Alun to labour long and hard, with prayer, spiritual exercise, and fasting, to keep his soul, to stay alive, not to succumb to the deadening effect of the form (if it was the form) of godliness without the power thereof.

Metcalfe begged Alun to keep experimental, in himself, and in fellowship, to avoid setting down the far side Jordan, in that which was not his rest, becoming contented with an apparently 'scriptural' outward appearance, which would surely leave his soul dry and lifeless, his testimony without power. Alun did not reply. Caught in the net, it appeared that he had taken offence, rejecting the word of exhortation and admonition.

Much time elapsed. Metcalfe now had been ordained to the Ministry, and, after some years, was called again to preach at large. Not until this period had passed did he receive the two letters which follow, very shortly after the last of which Alun Barton departed this life to be with the Saviour:

A. Barton,
Rhos-on-Sea,
N. Wales.

15th September, 1967

Dear Brother,

Looking at the 'Christian Herald' today, and particularly the 'Crusading for Christ' I saw your name, as one who will minister at Dudley, and I thought it would be a good idea to send my prayers and blessing to you on this occasion.

Do you remember me? It's nigh on twelve years since you spoke to me, in fact March 5th 1955 (it's marked in my bible), and you pointed me to One who *has* kept and undertaken, since that time. I have still got some of your letters and sometimes take them out to read, and, without exception, your warnings and prophecies of the pitfalls one may expect have been true, for indeed it has been a hard way, but I have proved Him, and the heartbreak and disappointments just pale to nothing when one considers our election and assurance of salvation.

I often think of you, and when I am called to speak and testify your name inevitably comes to mind. I trust the Lord will bless your ministry, be assured of the prayers of us 'few' in this part of the vineyard.

I go to the Mission at Llandudno (Independent). Mr. H.R. Jones is pastor, and we have a time of real spiritual blessing. How I praise Him, for His revealing to me the things of Himself. Brother, I had rather be a doorkeeper in the house of my God, than dwell in the tents of wickedness.

At the moment I am awaiting a visit to the Llandudno hospital of a heart specialist, (would you pray for me) and am being wonderfully sustained through the Lord's people praying and interceding.

You probably will be up to date with Bob Williams who gave his heart to the Lord under your ministry the same time as I. He has not found it easy, and has experienced a very difficult time.

I am closing now, do drop me a line if you have a few minutes, it will be lovely to hear from you. May God bless you and those who labour with you in your work, that many may be won for Christ, for He and He alone can save. Duw ach bendithio chwi.

Christian love,

Alun

A. Barton,
Rhos-on-Sea,
N. Wales.

Tuesday

My Dear John,

I feel I should answer your letter, as soon as possible, in view of my having to see the specialist and the opportunity may not present itself as favourably as at present.

First of all, to answer what to me was your very important question, my own view of the present state in spiritual affairs. Well, John, first and foremost the Lord Jesus Christ is more *precious* and *desirable* to all those who are born again, and secondly, looking forward to the Rapture, I Corinthians 15 verse 52, and I Thessalonians 4 verses 16 and 17. One can but look out on the present 'scene' and find systems breaking down, men in fear, unable to stand sound doctrine because of their sins; denominations and places of worship where the true, Spirit taught word is rejected; these are all passing away. I *personally cannot* have any part of it, for I believe we should be

17

with those who have been 'secured' and are linked to Christ by the precious blood.

You say it is a 'path of thorns'. May I refer you to Matthew 27 verses 28, 29 and 30. Yes it is the only way, for there is no compromise. We must be established in the Person and truth of the Lord, and raise up a standard thereby.

We, that is a few who are longing for that Holy Spirit fellowship, meet with one another, in our homes, just reading the word, praying and meditating, and oh, dear John, what impressions we receive. There are many, who had started, fallen away, but those who love Him and look for His appearing press on toward the mark of the high calling.

Sounds as if you are on these lines. I pray God's anointing on your ministry, and that He may use you to lead others to Him. I have not seen Bob Williams for a long time. I believe he could not go on in the ministry of the Presbyterian church and is now teaching.

David Shepherd, the Welsh evangelist is at Abergele. They are holding a ten day campaign, but I have been unable to support it, but some of my Christian friends call, and give me the 'low down'.

I have the joy of speaking on the Lord's Day, occasionally, then at the Open Air, and to testify and sing in certain towns, so I feel the Lord is using me.

So, John Bâch, be encouraged, if things appear dark, we are witnessing mighty things, and must hold fast to what we have, but we are not as ones without hope, for your own words to me twelve years ago were that Christ had *bridged* the gulf that sin had separated, and are now reconciled by His death.

18

I am closing now, but did want you to receive this epistle as soon as possible. God bless you and keep, strengthen and sustain you until I see you face to face.

Christian love in Him,
Alun

Some Remarkable Conversions

THE memory of some now gathered in one of the oldest congregations raised up through the preaching of the gospel of the grace of God, reaches back almost to the beginning of Mr. Metcalfe's ministry, when they were saved under the powerful preaching of the gospel in 1955. They have been under this ministry ever since. These men and women know and testify of the power of the Spirit in Mr. Metcalfe and of his unblemished life and character to this self-same day.

They have seen the work of God through more than three decades and the sure marks of a true minister of Christ, in a man who has walked in integrity and truth, despite many sore domestic trials, troubles and persecutions.

These older brethren and sisters have been kept by the power of God and are a witness to much 'fruit that remains', standing to this very day as a testimony to the power that is in the gospel. These first heard Mr. Metcalfe preach in April 1955 and felt for the first time in their experience the power of the Holy Ghost under the anointing of the Spirit of God. As the fifth chapter of the gospel of John was opened and Christ was preached, their hearts burned within them. All were gripped by a deep conviction as the Spirit applied the truth that this was the word of the Lord. None had heard it on this wise before: the deep impressions of those times have remained until this day and all that has happened since then has but served to strengthen the depth of that first love. To God be the glory and praise.

Mr. Metcalfe was then a young man who had been saved only three years before. God had already given him a wisdom in the ways of the Lord beyond his years, and his knowledge of God's word and his exposition of the scriptures were outstanding. From the day of his conversion he had found within himself a deep hunger and thirst which had caused him to cry out, 'as the hart panteth after the water brooks, so panteth my soul after thee, O God.'

The bible, which he had never opened before, straightway became meat and drink to him and esteemed above his necessary food. Day after day he would read alone on his knees for hours, bathe every page with tears, and cover every word and sentence with prayer. After only three years his profiting appeared to all and it was plain that God had his hand on this man.

Before 1955, Mr. Metcalfe had been blessed in his preaching in small country chapels in Warwickshire. After this he served as an evangelist with a well known organisation. At the leading of the Holy Spirit—because of so much error in modern evangelism, both as to method and matter—he left this movement at a time when he was becoming well known, was preaching to hundreds, and souls were being saved.

The Lord showed his servant from the scriptures that the steady preaching and teaching of the word was the apostolic way in which souls were called and built up in the faith. After a series of providences, Mr. Metcalfe was asked to preach in a Congregational church as a pulpit supply on one occasion. This was where many first heard him preach with such great power. Three months later, after remarkable providences, signs and direct answers to prayer, he was called to minister in that place.

Revival followed the preaching of the gospel in the power of the Holy Ghost. Many were saved at that time in demonstration of the Spirit and of power, some in connection with remarkable circumstances which drew them to come under the preaching of the word for the first time, being instantly called by the voice of the Son of God.

One example of this divine moving appeared in the case of an old tramp, really a dreaming romantic, who had spent a lifetime wandering over the moors and wild places of England, the hills and mountains of Wales, travelling on little known and less used byways and paths, always searching, searching for some elusive dream which the wild places seemed to promise but never fulfilled.

The dream beckoned always just beyond the hills, the other side of the mountains, ever beyond the horizon: never realised. Now at the end of his days, strangely (he knew not why) the old tramp was drawn to travel through unfamiliar and long detested built-up areas, to a town he would never otherwise have visited, having no idea what he was doing or why he had come: only an uncanny compulsion moved him he knew not where.

Passing through streets abhorrent to his nature and foreign to his wild haunts, walking onwards and onwards, as it fell out one evening (it was a Sunday) he came to the place where the preaching of the gospel had commenced. He was rooted to the spot. The moving impulse ceased within him. He knew that he had arrived. Deep in his soul he sensed that he should enter, and enter such a place for the first time in his life. He knew by instinct that this place at that time was the cause of his feet being turned despite himself to such unfamiliar surroundings.

All through the previous week John Metcalfe could get no word from the Lord to preach for that evening. He was shut up, and the heavens were as brass, even to the hour of assembly. After the preliminary service, the time appointed for preaching came, but his heart was utterly empty, his soul stone cold: nothing came from the Lord.

Torn with anxiety, almost physically sick with apprehension, Metcalfe rose as if to speak yet having nothing to say. Literally at that very moment the pilgrimage of the children of Israel was profoundly impressed upon his heart. He opened his bible and his mouth on the words, 'Give ear, O Shepherd of Israel'. He noticed nothing of the quiet entry of the old tramp at the rear of the crowded congregation, for just as John Metcalfe in his soul distress rose to speak from he knew not what, so the old man entered. And as the old man stood still, so the word of the Lord came to the preacher.

As a man inspired, Mr. Metcalfe preached as if he had been transported back those thousands of years, and was describing what he saw and felt as if it were unfolding then and there before his very eyes. Equally inspired, the congregation seemed to see and feel with him. It was as if all felt the spray whipped from the towering waves of the Red Sea, parted on either side, as Israel passed over dryshod to the far side. The tramp of marching feet, punctuated by the crashing of the waves as the waters returned behind them, seemed to resound from wall to wall of the building.

Indeed, so transfixed were both preacher and congregation under the power and presence of the Holy Ghost in the preaching of the word that to them the building faded, the vast desert sky appeared to hang over the heads of the people whilst the winds howling out of the wilderness seemed to sting the eyes from the flying grains of sand whipped from the trackless desert wastes reaching from far horizon to far horizon.

This was the pilgrimage from the land of Egypt to the promised land. Ahead loomed the pillar of cloud by day, and the pillar of fire by night, as God marched in the wilderness, the Shepherd of Israel through the howling wastes, leading the pilgrims, strangers and sojourners, out of this world to the land that is very far off.

As never before the eyes of the old tramp were a fountain of tears. His worn, weather-beaten face was wet with weeping. His soul was stirred to depths beyond him to contain. All this he knew in his experience, but what he experienced for the first time, that the wild places, the ragged rocks, and the howling wastes could never tell him, and never did tell him, was the way to the promised land, the purpose of this passing pilgrimage, and the existence of a rest that remained to the people of God.

These things were in the prerogative of the Shepherd of Israel, who drew near, seeming invisibly to tap the shoulder of the old man that night, as if to say, 'This is the way; walk ye in it.' This voice he knew to be the voice of the Shepherd, and that hand on his shoulder he felt to be nail pierced.

The old man went out that night with a mighty outspoken confession, truly regenerate, the light of the glory bright on his countenance, a pilgrim and a stranger on the earth, who at last knew what he had sought, where it was to be found, and who it was that would lead him there.

For now, as he witnessed before leaving, he sought a country, that is, an heavenly; and he sought a city, a glorious city, whose builder and maker is God. This only should be his rest, and he knew it was through the atonement of the Lamb of God, it was by the resurrection from the dead, and it was certain and secure in the world to come. This was the testimony that came from his own mouth as he departed, full of joy and peace, that evening.

Next follows the account of another remarkable conversion. Remarkable also, because it concerns not the many young people brought under the power of God in the gospel at that time, but another person of great age, one of those for whom the time might have seemed past, for whom it appeared too late.

An old lady, very frail indeed, unable to walk or stand, had heard of the visitation of the Spirit in the Chapel, for it was noised abroad.

As a young woman in the latter half of the previous century she had been spoken to and convicted of God in a Salvation Army meeting. In the appeal to come forward to the 'penitent's bench', as it was called, she responded, going to the front to seek Christ and to yield her heart and life to him.

Alas, almost immediately, the love of the world came in, the love of Christ went out, and instead she sought for love from other quarters altogether. From that time as a young woman in the late 1800's, to this day well over half a century later, she never again raised so much as a thought to her salvation, or darkened the doors of a place of worship.

Now, ancient and frail, she had heard of the moving of the Holy Ghost in the meetings, and, in consequence, had been cut to the heart with remorse. Weeping over the wastage of her life, unable to move, she was convicted by the Holy Ghost, who stirred her irresistibly to seek that somehow she should hear the word of God before she died.

Resolved in her heart to come, her determination set, she begged her neighbours to bring her. And brought she was, wheeled in her chair to the meeting. She sat weeping throughout the mighty preaching of the word even to the close, as, in the breathless and awesome hush of eternity which followed, the voice of many weepers was heard.

Another sound intervened, the sound of a wheelchair being pushed up the aisle by a deacon at her importunate insistence. So the frail old woman, now some ninety years of age, re-enacted her calling upon the Lord in that Salvation Army meeting so long ago. The Lord had broken her heart with one look from his eyes, and she found her pardon written within by the finger of God. The word was, 'Return unto the LORD thy God; for thou hast fallen by thine iniquity. Take with you words, and turn to the LORD: say unto him, Take away all iniquity, and receive us graciously', Hosea 14:1,2.

So she returned, though with her vessel empty, and found abundant mercy and free grace in the day of her visitation. Within the week she had gone to glory.

At this time many were convicted of their sin, so powerfully that strong men could not find the strength even to stand on their feet, so convinced were they of that great and terrible day of the Lord, when all shall be required to render an account of every deed done in the body and of every idle word spoken.

How every word from the Lord struck home, causing much fallow ground to be broken up, so that many hard hearts were pierced and melted. Many cast away their empty, false professions, vain hopes and dead works. The brittle joy and all the over-confidence and zeal of youth were dissolved in the sight of a Holy God before whom nothing stood but the work of his own hands.

Souls were driven out of their refuges of lies and hiding places, the barriers of years were broken down, and many fled to Christ for salvation. There was a tremendous sense of the imminence of the Lord's return—'behold the Judge' stood 'at the door'—and there was an earnest looking for the return of Christ, together with a great longing for the world to come.

At the close of the meetings the atmosphere was indescribable, no one daring to move for the great power that filled the place. All consciousness of time was lost, only the sense of eternity was present.

The fear of God came upon all the people, man, woman, and young child alike, and that not just in the meetings. What tears were shed in prayer, what answers to prayer were given, and how the Lord was praised for his goodness and mercy in raising up his word and work in these last days. Nothing would ever be the same again for the hearers, whether they would hear or forbear. Truly, this was a savour of life unto life and of death unto death.

The love of Christ was manifest in the preaching and the King set forth in his beauty. The world was forgotten and the Saviour longed for. All was so vivid and the freshness of this time of the Lord's visitation abides until this moment in the hearts of those that remain; a number who were saved then have already gone to be with Christ.

There were other marks of a work of God. Nothing was allowed to come between one and another; nothing was left in the ground lest it should spring up to grieve the Spirit and spoil the unity. Truly it could be said 'see how they love one another'. And they loved the Lord's servant, who brought the living word to those dead in trespasses and sins. That this work might spread, all took cheerfully the spoiling of their goods, and no one looked upon anything as their own—all was for Christ.

The Sowing in Tears

IT soon became plain, under the leading and teaching of the Holy Spirit, that it was not only a revival of religion that was needed in these last days but a reformation also, and that not back to the reformers, godly men though they were, nor to some past work once raised up of God, nor to man's books however edifying, but right back to the beginning, to the new testament and then not to copy the letter but to seek the grace of life, to walk in the same light and power and to worship God in the same spirit and truth as those under the apostles in the beginning.

When the Lord revealed to his servant the need for a reformation, Mr. Metcalfe pursued this vision with his whole heart. Not all obeyed the gospel and although the building was filled with hearers both on the first day of the week and in the midweek meetings, nevertheless at the sound and practice of a thorough reformation of the church many began to turn away from Christ and reject his servant. What then appeared to be the hurtful rejection by man, was in reality the work of God. The Lord's servant, together with some of the converts who followed him as he followed Christ, was cast on him who said, 'I will never leave thee nor forsake thee' and 'Lo, I am with you alway, even unto the end of the world.'

Other sure marks of the true, sent ministry appeared. Afflictions and persecutions were seen to be the portion of the Lord's servant, as they are, in a measure, the lot of all who would live godly in Christ Jesus. The Spirit led Mr. Metcalfe by a lonely path to partake of the afflictions of the gospel, in obscurity, ostracisation, false accusation, the ridicule of some and much misunderstanding from others, to say nothing of the inward pressures, the loneliness, and the more patent outward burdens of poverty and at times the loss of all things. This was surely the sowing in tears.

There were two specific periods in the course of Mr. Metcalfe's ministry when he was shut up alone to seek God in watching and prayer, and in the diligent study of the word of God. The first of these periods lasted seven years, the latter three years. In the seven year period the Lord burdened his servant with many questions about the doctrine of Christ and with the pressing need to search out the truth from the scriptures alone.

During these years when he was shut up to this work, God gave his servant great insight into the word of God, on his knees, or more often on his face, crying to the Lord to open the book. He studied long hours by day and often by night, to the detriment of his health and eyes, determined 'to know the doctrine' and having grasped it, to hold it fast lest at any time it should be let slip. These years have borne abundant fruit and God has since enabled Mr. Metcalfe to preach these essential and precious truths and to publish them abroad by means of his books.

The Reaping in Joy

AFTER the seven year period of solitary study, in obedience to the Lord's leading by signs and providences afforded to his servant, a door was opened for Mr. Metcalfe to render a testimony to thousands both in the U.K. and in Europe.

He became well known as an evangelist and teacher and many sought to have him preach in their pulpits and on their platforms. A great number of souls were saved at this time and these are still standing, although some have departed to be with Christ.

Those whose hearts were touched remember every detail of the meetings and above all the messages. There are many letters and testimonies to the way in which the word of life was received. The preaching 'breathed the very spirit of the New Testament.' 'We have been thrilled beyond words at what our ears have heard and at what our eyes have seen.' 'Our church will never be the same again.' 'How he presented the messages with thoroughness and truth!' 'His words remain in our hearts.'

The following example from among the many articles in the Christian press at that time will suffice to show the remarkable spiritual effect and converting power that accompanied Mr. Metcalfe's ministry:

The Christian Newspaper, November 1965

JOHN METCALFE'S MISSION
BY THE REV. PETER BARBER

Who is John Metcalfe? What is he like? How does he preach? These were the questions that circulated in East Kilbride Baptist Church when we heard that John Metcalfe,

Evangelist with the Movement for World Evangelization, was to come to us in place of David Shepherd, who had been taken ill.

Only two things we then knew about him ... that he had a remarkable conversion, and that he had spent eight years of his life, living by faith, devoting himself exclusively to an exhaustive study of the Bible. Which things made us wonder. Startling conversions can produce fanatical zealots; monastic study can create detached mystics.

Who was this John Metcalfe?

From the moment we met him, we liked him. He was modest, yet friendly and with a quick sense of humour. He was extremely well informed, yet devoid of narrow-minded dogmatism. He was willing to learn and eager to please. His love of God's word and devotion to Christ had done nothing to make him remote from men. We sensed that we were in the presence of a man of God.

From the moment we heard him preach, we knew that John Metcalfe was different. Here was preaching in the great apostolic tradition. It breathed the very spirit of the New Testament.

There was authority in his every utterance, and even the casual asides were fresh and illuminating. There was a compelling intensity as God's servant presented Christ in all the majesty of his Person, and in all the magnificence of his work. Every doctrine found its focus in Christ, the Christ of God. It was a profoundly moving experience to sit and listen.

He did not evade the major doctrines of the difficult themes so basic to the gospel. He preached on eternal life, justification, the atonement, the Last Supper, the substitutionary death, the evangel.

But this was no dull, dry exposition. The truths proclaimed had so gripped John Metcalfe's heart and mind that they lit a fire of glowing appreciation in the soul of those who listened. And the sheer immensity of the truths he portrayed filled us with a sense of awe. And yet, withal, there was clarity and simplicity in each message, so that even young teenagers could understand his teaching. (I checked on this, and can vouch that it is true.)

This is evangelism in a new dimension ... not so much evangelism by appeal as *evangelism by instruction*. There is nothing trivial or superficial about it. Before ever the will is challenged, the mind is informed ... fully and lucidly.

The effect of such evangelism surpasses anything I have before experienced. Not only have numbers grown night by night, with people of all ages and of all kinds attending, but decisions are being registered that stagger and thrill us. Both church adherents and complete outsiders are accepting Christ, and many backsliders have been restored. But the deepest work of all is quite unseen.

This mission has not only been a mission by the church, but at the same time a mission *to* the church. It is quite impossible to keep abreast of the spread of the blessing within the church membership.

Everyone seems to have come into a new awareness of the glory of Christ and the greatness of the gospel. Lives are being fully surrendered; a hunger for the word of God has been created; preachers among us are being humbled at the realisation of how utterly unworthy their own presentation of Christ has been; a number of members have spontaneously requested a half-night of prayer right in the midst of the mission.

What we have come to see is that teaching and evangelism are not two separate compartments. John Metcalfe is supremely a teacher, but surely best described as a teacher-Evangelist. It is not evangelism or teaching, but evangelism through teaching. We are confident that the fruit of such an evangelism is bound to remain. Its very basis is the truth.

We have been thrilled beyond words at what our ears have heard and at what our eyes have seen. Our church will never be the same again. We can only say ... 'There was a man sent from God, whose name was John'.

'The Christian'

November 5th, 1965

Back to the Wilderness

BUT the Lord had given John Metcalfe a great burden for the church, in response to which he returned to solitude for a second period, this time of three years, wrestling in prayer and studying the scriptures, completely giving himself to the work. The cost was literally heart-breaking. Through these periods of lonely vigil, first seven years and then three, besides other periods, there was also the search for others like-minded, who had in some measure walked the same path of obedient faith, had experienced the same power of the Holy Ghost, or had some real acquaintance with the way of suffering walked by all the true servants of God.

During this time of sowing there was the joy and blessing of having openings into the word, answers to prayer, the comfort of the Holy Ghost, and signs afforded to the Lord's servant that God was with him.

Those who met together over these years remember them with joy. What a privilege to be among those who feared the Lord, who spake often one to another. Many meetings are recalled as times of heaven on earth and all wanted to hold on to the moment and not part or go home.

Although Mr. Metcalfe spent so many years shut up to the continuous study of God's word with such single-minded devotion, he is not like some dull academic or religious recluse.

He is intolerant of evil, hypocrisy or cant and impatient with time-wasting trivialities and slipshod service especially in the things of God. He has a kindly sense of humour and is a good friend who 'loveth at all times'. All who meet him are immediately made at ease by his warmth and friendliness and his interest in others.

There is nothing remote or hard about him and his sufferings for the sake of the gospel have not made him bitter or narrow-minded. He is transparently open and willing to share his wide experience, very approachable and ready to help all who need his counsel in spiritual things or in practical matters. Mr. Metcalfe never 'talks down' to anyone even to the youngest, and is always eager to profit from the experience of another. He is beloved of all.

Bethlehem: 'The House of Bread'

THE path of the true minister of the gospel is always marked by prayer, and prayer that is answered. This has been abundantly evident during the years that are past and is still so in the Lord's dealings with his servant. In 1968, Mr. Metcalfe was moved to ask the Lord for a small Methodist chapel in Tylers Green where he lived, although there was no question of its being on the market. Some time later he heard that it was going to be sold.

He again sought the Lord to provide the means to buy it: he was heard and answered. Although a number of other interested people bid for the building, Mr. Metcalfe's offer for the place was accepted. This building is now Bethlehem Meeting Hall which was opened after extensive renovation in January 1969 and is the meeting place of what is, so far, the largest of the congregations gathered in the United Kingdom.

However, there were only a few saints there in 1969, five men and a few women. God blessed the work greatly and it so increased that enlargement was required, then it increased again until this day when the place is filled.

Many have been born again in this Meeting Hall by the power of the Holy Spirit through the preaching of the word of God.

Typical of these present day conversions of the new testament kind are those which follow in sequence, selected at random from a company of whom it is evidently true that 'Ye are manifestly declared to be the epistle of Christ ministered by us, written not with ink, but with the Spirit of the living God; not in tables of stone, but in fleshy tables of the heart.'

The Conversion of Tamsin Ginger

From Tamsin Ginger,
Tylers Green,
Buckinghamshire.

31st March, 1990

I was brought up to believe that God is, but no more than that. I felt nothing of my sins, and so felt no need of deliverance, until I was about fifteen years old. Even then, when I began to attend a Baptist church, my motives were far more social than spiritual. From time to time I was stirred, especially when reading the scriptures. But these stirrings were swiftly quietened by the easy reassurances from the Baptist pulpit.

I went on in this way, with so little thought for God or concern for my soul, for three years. Then I left the Baptist church. Over the next few years I occasionally attended different places, feeling a hunger after God which I knew could never be satisfied in any of them.

Gradually these shallow sensations ceased and for several years I was completely taken up with my own things and not with the things of God. But, praise the name of the LORD, he had not given me up. He was not in all my thoughts, but he did not leave me in my way of sin and condemnation.

I began to feel something of the burden of my sins, I longed to hear of Christ, I longed for salvation. I knew that I was not saved and that everything I had professed before had been without foundation. I searched the scriptures for the first time in years. I longed to meet with God's people, but I knew that I could not bear to go back to the Baptist church. Then, through one of the brethren at work, I learnt of the Bethlehem Meeting Hall.

At the first meeting I attended, in Autumn 1984, I knew in my heart that those gathered were God's people. I was stirred by the things I heard, and professed conversion. Shortly afterwards I was baptized.

I went on then for several months, believing myself to be saved. But I was complacent, and in the Spring of 1985 I was shaken from my complacency to realise that my 'conversion' had been but the beginning of God's work in my soul.

Now I felt the fear of God, the force of the law, and the knowledge of my sin. I was crushed and bowed down, knowing the impossibility of my pleasing God. I knew now that salvation belongeth unto the LORD, and that he has mercy on whom he will. If he did not save me, then I would not be saved. I sought the LORD with many tears, that his goodness would lead me to repentance.

The preaching of the gospel by the Lord's servant was more precious to me than it ever had been, and it was under the preaching, from Ephesians 4, that I was saved. I thank God, who gave his Son, our Lord Jesus Christ, to suffer for me and to bear my sins in his body. With the psalmist, I love the

LORD, because he hath heard my voice and my supplications. He delivered my soul from death, mine eyes from tears, and my feet from falling.

From the first time I came to the Bethlehem Meeting Hall my husband, Stuart, was very much against my attendance. He had already been turned against Mr. Metcalfe by members of Mr. Metcalfe's family, and when I continued to meet with the saints he was very angry and sometimes violent. I had a set of Mr. Metcalfe's books in the house and one stormy night Stuart threw them all out in the rain onto the wet grass.

On another occasion, determined to find out more about the 'cult' at Tylers Green, he climbed over the fence in the middle of a meeting and demanded entrance. The Lord sustained me on these and many other occasions, and the fellowship of the saints was a great comfort to me. I prayed for Stuart, but truly with little faith, and I was very encouraged when others said that they also prayed for him.

Nearly a year after my conversion, Stuart's father died, which deeply affected Stuart. For the first time he thought of his own death. He asked to see one of the saints, and, by the grace of God, was turned from idols to serve the living and true God.

The change in Stuart was abrupt, and he began to attend the meetings, hearing the gospel for the first time, and worshipping God in the gathering of the saints.

I am so thankful for the Lord's mercy to me. O magnify the LORD with me, and let us exalt his name together. I sought the LORD, and he heard me, and delivered me from all my fears.

Tamsin Ginger

The Conversion of
Stuart Twitchen

From Stuart Twitchen,
Tylers Green,
Buckinghamshire.

My upbringing was by no means religious, although I was encouraged to attend Sunday school, and there was some acknowledgement of a Christian God. However, even from an early age I remember having some sense of God and Jesus Christ, accepting that what I was taught of Jesus was true. At about aged twelve I left the local Sunday school and any sense of things to do with God left me. I rebelled against God and my parents and all authority and sought to fulfil my own desires. This began a period in my life in which I believe, had not the Lord in his mercy preserved my life, I would have destroyed it.

The means of temporary respite from my state at that time was by my making a profession and 'accepting Jesus'. I became an active member of a Baptist church and found that I could do nearly all the things I did when 'unconverted', but still be 'converted'. I know now my conscience was seared with a hot iron (I Timothy 4:2). I had many friends at the Baptist church who had been brought up as 'Christians', and others who had come along via youth groups etc. In fact everyone was embraced who made a profession or who had some tenuous connection with religion.

I believe there was no discernment in these matters or any taking earnest heed to the truth of the gospel of Jesus Christ. Truly the blind led the blind, and I loved to have it so. All my religion stood in my decision to accept or reject it. This was what I was taught and this I gladly accepted, and professed the same to others also.

Eventually I saw the deadness of my profession and how hypocritical I had become, trying to live a religious life but knowing the more I tried the more I failed. Even in that dreadful apostate and hypocritical state not once was I warned of judgment and the wrath of God, 'For the wrath of God is revealed from heaven against all ungodliness and unrighteousness of men, who hold the truth in unrighteousness' (Romans 1:18). This was my condition; I was blind, dead, full of unrighteousness and unable to do a thing about it. But in this church all this was tolerated and I was never brought to account for my sins, no not by them.

But the Lord did not forsake me, for he chastens and leads his people by a way they know not, for 'Salvation is of the LORD' (Psalm 3:8). So I renounced all my religious commitment and returned (although it was hardly returning for I was virtually in it anyway) wholeheartedly to the world.

I was gripped by ambition and striving for money and a certain status and threw my whole effort into work and fulfilling the lusts of the heart. How true it is when the apostle describes the things that are in the world (I John 2:16), the lust of the flesh, the lust of the eye and the pride of life. These things were fulfilled in me. My whole life was for myself. I had no thoughts for God or his rights and I despised religion. Just before I left every form of religion I met my wife, Tamsin, and this was also a contributing factor to leaving the church. For we both felt no desire to continue going so we both stopped.

And, no doubt, had not the Lord intervened we would have carried on believing that all things continue as they were from the beginning (II Peter 3:4). But in 1984 Tamsin began to attend Bethlehem Meeting Hall at Tylers Green. My first reaction was one of acceptance. When she first told me she was going to the meeting I paid little attention. It wasn't for me: but who was I to stop her going to church? I thought that once she had gone and seen that it was like all the other churches we had been to she would have nothing to do with it. But little did I know how the flesh would strive against the Spirit when there was a true work of God being done.

After her first meeting I asked a few questions but did not take much interest. But soon she was attending all the weekday and weekend meetings which began to encroach into my time. My tolerance soon evaporated and I exerted my energies to prevent her attending the meetings.

I knew two of Mr. Metcalfe's family and sought advice or information about the meeting. From the information given me, by one in particular, my perception of Mr. Metcalfe and the brethren at Bethlehem was so distorted, with what I now know to be complete and utter lies, that my anger was all the more fuelled to prevent my wife from being involved with such people.

Although I had misgivings about these lies I chose to believe them (II Thess. 2:11,12). I had pleasure in unrighteousness. With this in mind and the thought that I was losing my wife to some sect (Acts 28:22) I strove even the more against her, but she would not, and had I known it, could not, yield to my demands and forsake the true and living God. I seemed to be taken up with this task to undermine the work that had begun in her.

On one occasion I pulled all the books and tracts written by Mr. Metcalfe from the bookshelf and threw them out of the house; on another I broke furniture and stormed with rage. At these times I became almost mad with fury, and I know now that principalities and powers that then I knew nothing about motivated me to act as I did. Often I would fly into a rage and enmity would rise in my heart. How the heart is deceitful above all things, and desperately wicked: who can know it? (Jeremiah 17:9).

One time I went to Bethlehem Meeting Hall during a first-day evening meeting and demanded entry. This act prompted Mr. Metcalfe to intervene and so it was arranged that he should visit Tamsin and me at our home. I had never met Mr. Metcalfe before which was curious considering I had such strong opinions of him. But there were many opponents of his ministry who claimed to be religious to whom I turned for help or advice. These all had a sympathetic and listening ear to my plight, opposing Mr. Metcalfe. This was despite the fact that their judgments were based on hearsay without once having met Mr. Metcalfe themselves, or having once known his manner of life by their own observation (II Timothy 3:10,11). They preferred to believe lies rather than the true witness of those who had been delivered from the depths of despair, the testimony of many who once were blind but now could see. For Mr. Metcalfe is surely a servant sent of God to a hungry and thirsty people.

From the first time I met Mr. Metcalfe I found it hard to accept the outlandish things spoken against him. It was obvious, although I would not allow myself to believe it, that the man I saw and spoke to was completely opposite to the image which evil speakers had led me to believe of him. I could not agree with his religion, and, in my arrogance, and to my shame, I laughed at his godly manner and faithful testimony. But despite this, having met him, I felt relieved and easier with the situation concerning my wife's attending the meetings.

It was not until 1986 that events occurred that would lead me to abhor myself in dust and ashes and cry to the Lord for mercy. That year my father died and I was very much affected by this loss. It caused me to look within myself and question my state before God. As with the psalmist my heart was sore pained within me, and the terrors of death were fallen upon me (Psalm 55:4,5). The sorrows of death engulfed me (Psalm 116:3) and the more I tried to escape the realisation of the inevitability of my own death the more I was troubled, and at times beside myself with fear. I had no one to turn to who could stop this enemy. All my rationalising and theorising were no help here. I feared for my very life.

This continued for some time, then one evening while in a severe state of anxiety and fear that gripped me in a way I had never known before, there became impressed upon me my awful and dreadful condition before God. I felt my soul had been given up and there was no hope for me with God or man. What terrible sensations came upon me as I perceived that a place of death and judgment awaited me for my wicked and ungodly life. How could I break from this, as I deserved all that was due to me? How dark and deep in despair I sank.

I asked Tamsin if she could ask someone from the meeting to visit me. Through her, John Darroch came to visit, for Mr. Metcalfe was in the Far East preaching. John Darroch listened to me as I spoke of my fears and my feeling of utter helplessness. I knew then that if I were to die that night then I would be lost, without God and condemned to eternal damnation, for I knew this was my just reward for my sin before God. So how could I, after all my behaviour, possibly be just with God? How could I, whose wickedness had gone before me, expect mercy? The answer was—with man this is impossible but with God all things are possible. This was the word that caused hope to spring into my heart: 'Whosoever calleth upon the name of the Lord shall be saved.'

For the first time I felt the presence of the Lord, this word came with power also. I prayed and poured my heart out to him and he answered me with a witness. The scales fell from my eyes, my heart was rent, and with fear and trembling I felt the peace that passeth all understanding enter my soul, and I felt the burden of sin and the fear of that last great enemy, death, leave me, as the daystar arose in my heart.

O Blessed Saviour! for salvation, of a truth, is all of the Lord.

I bear witness to the faithful remnant at Bethlehem Meeting Hall, as I do to the selfless ministry of the Lord's servant, Mr. Metcalfe. How blind I had been, but thanks be to God for Christ opened my blind eyes, so that now I see!

I cannot but bear witness to the things I have seen and heard. Especially I want to speak to those religious that were so keen, in my unconverted state, to support me in my ignorance as I railed against this sent gospel ministry. But even though I can testify to God's dealings with me they still will not relent.

Now I sincerely believe that even if a man was raised from the dead before their very eyes, they would not believe (Luke 16:31). For in their wisdom they become fools (Rom. 1:22), as I was when in my sad and wicked state.

But now the winter is past, (Song 2:11-13), and my hard heart is melted. For I was drawn to the Son by the Father, that I may know him, and believe on him, who gave himself a propitiation for my sins, so that I might worship the Father in Spirit and in truth with all those whom he purchased with his own blood. And, knowing that I have been forgiven much, by his grace I love much, knowing that I have passed from death unto life because I love the brethren. Amen.

Stuart Twitchen

A Dying Testimony: Mrs. Elizabeth Bain

from her daughter Moira Darroch

In view of her love towards the Lord Jesus and her steadfast determination to be found only in the truth, I thought it might be an encouragement to others if they were to know something of the closing days upon earth of my mother, Mrs. Elizabeth Bain.

My mother was born in Glasgow in 1916, where she continued to reside for all but the last nine years of her life, these final years being happily spent in fellowship with the saints meeting at Bethlehem Meeting Hall, Tylers Green.

Converted to Christ, out of the world, at the age of twenty-two, she began regularly to attend the crowded meetings at the Tent Hall, Steel Street, where Jock Troup was then the superintendent.

Later, she was for many years in fellowship with Open Brethren, but at length becoming disappointed with the lack of real food for her soul, my mother finally left their assemblies in 1963. Finding this failure in the ministry not confined to Brethren, but widespread, she removed from Glasgow in 1979, to be under the ministry and care of Mr. Metcalfe, knowing, through his having visited that city on a number of occasions, the demonstration of the Spirit and of power that attended his preaching.

Here she felt that the Lord had at last led her to the house of her Master's brethren, and her great delight was to be found at all the meetings of the saints.

In the early part of this year (1988) her health began noticeably to decline and she was eventually admitted to hospital. Some months prior to her illness, and almost as if she knew that it would be her last opportunity, she had begun to re-read every one of Mr. Metcalfe's books in sequence, completing her reading of them only a few weeks before her death.

The day after my mother was taken into hospital, the enemy sought to take advantage of her extreme physical weakness, and, through his accusations, caused her, for a short time, to doubt her salvation. But the Lord sustained her, and she was able to say to me that evening, 'It's all clear now. It's not of man. It's all of God. God has done the whole work.' Moments later she said, 'Mr. Metcalfe preaches the truth, he has been sent of God.' Then, repeating a few times, 'Not of man; not of works, lest any man should boast. It's the grace of God that brings salvation. It's all of grace.'

Two days later, very early in the morning, she suddenly broke out with these words, 'I love the Lord, because he first loved me and gave himself for me.' After quoting a number of texts from Isaiah 53, she then said, 'He hath loved us with an *everlasting* love.' She continued in this joyful frame for some time, many texts concerning the love and mercy of God to sinners coming to her lips. Then, beckoning her sister and myself to her bedside, she said, 'Moira, Maisie, In all thy ways acknowledge him and he shall direct thy paths.'

The following day, again very early, she was found engaged in audible prayer. Standing on the brink of eternity, her final concern was for the testimony of Jesus on earth. Unaware of anyone's presence, she continued to call upon the Lord from morning till evening. Surely these words of her travail must find an echo in the heart of every saint who looks for a return of the glory:

'Oh, Father, send a miracle. How parched and dry we are! Cause them to know that thou art the living God, the Maker of all things. Save thy people from their sins. Raise up thy holy temple. Save men and women by thy gospel which thy faithful servant has preached for years. Men have tried to drown thy word, but, please, please raise it up again by thy faithful servant Mr. Metcalfe. Let thy name be glorified in the earth. Let thy name be magnified in all the earth by that Man, Christ Jesus.'

The last words spoken by my mother expressed that she wished to be with the Lord. Very soon after, on 4th May, 1988, her desire was granted, and she passed through death into life to be with him whom her soul loveth.

Moira Darroch

The Conversion of Nigel Johnstone

Church Road,
Tylers Green.
30th December, 1972

I am writing to give an account of my testimony and also of the preaching which played such a memorable part in this work. I didn't write before because there was no sudden change, and, because of my unbelief and hardening of my heart, the laying of my soul down in trust upon the mercy and grace of the Lord Jesus Christ was drawn out.

I was first awakened to the reality of eternity and death and thus the dawning realisation that I needed to be right with God and men when I was about seven years of age. The thoughts kept flashing across my mind, as though a match flared in my soul before spluttering out, 'Who am I?'; 'Why am I here?'; 'Why are things as they are?'.

I carried on through a semi-religious childhood, my father being a minister of the Scottish kirk, encouraged to believe that I was good and even better than others. When I was about twelve, I began to feel the unreality of the world, as if it was all like a thin smear of paint on a canvas, which I might tear away and find a greater reality behind.

I also began to fear death, not for myself, at that time, but I wondered what it would be like if one or both of my parents died. I felt it would be such a loss, unable to see them any more and I realized what an awful, heart-rending thing it is for somebody to be no longer there.

It was also about this time that, because we had moved to a new area, I was without close friends and felt a keen sense of loneliness for a few years, my family circumstances aggravating this to give a sense of being unwanted.

I used to listen to the radio and heard Garner Ted Armstrong, leader of an heretical cult, speaking in an impressive way of God. I sent for some of his literature and one of his remarks struck me—it was that Christians shouldn't sin because, he said, 'the wages of sin is death'. I had previously thought to myself that if I 'believed' about Jesus Christ I would be all right for heaven and could then live as I liked, but, although that was good enough for the Church of Scotland, in which I had been brought up, it wasn't good enough for Garner Ted Armstrong. I think it was then that I felt the beginning of the fear so contrary to the materialistic religion which I had imbibed, for although eternity and death pressed harder and harder on my reason, yet I was full of false ideas and notions about the simplest of the things concerning God and my relationship with him.

I was at that time a 'known thief and liar', had a vile and blasphemous mouth and had God not arrested me, I have no doubt that despite a respectable upbringing I would have got worse and worse.

Through family connections I became more acquainted with religious people, but, although I behaved decently with them, I was very foul at school. I carried on a sort of double life for a long time excusing myself all the while. While on holiday with a religious group, I was sufficiently free from my worldly companions to pray to God that he would 'take my life' because I didn't want it, this being, I believe, mostly an irresponsible attitude to growing up. It was on this holiday that I met the first person who impressed me for religious zeal, and, having got acquainted, he took me to hear an American Evangelist. Under considerable emotional pressure, I was fifteen, and a desire to be the centre of attention, I went forward at his appeal although he had said almost nothing about the gospel. Afterwards, he prayed with the whole group of young people who had gone forward and allowed those who so desired to leave. I went, not realizing the significance attached to what I had done.

My acquaintance then introduced me to a Baptist church and since I believed it was the right thing to do, and since I saw how meaningless it was to be sprinkled as an infant, I went forward to be baptized. Becoming accepted, I was paired off, without effort on my part, with a girlfriend, of course also baptized, and took up an 'Evangelical Profession'.

I had no change of heart and deep down I knew that I loved the world and my sins more than I loved Christ, but this state seemed quite acceptable in the Evangelical circles in which I moved and so my earlier fears under Garner Ted Armstrong were stifled.

I became acquainted, through sources outside the Baptist church with what is termed 'Calvinism' and was told that man was totally evil by nature, that Christ had died for the sins of the elect only (and not everybody as was generally believed) that the elect had been chosen by God before they were born, and that their conversion and ultimate entrance to glory was certain despite themselves. I saw that these truths were more in line with what the scripture said and were more logical than the self-contradictory theories of 'General Ransom' and 'Free Will' and so I embraced them intellectually, though still quite without a change of heart.

I grew more and more religious in an external way yet more and more worldly in an internal way, still in my double life, yet more vociferous about the Bible, which I hardly read in private, having no love for the word of God. I went on a 'campaign' to a holiday resort and there, seizing the opportunity of getting behind a microphone, bawled about 'sin' and 'the blood' on street corners, knowing almost nothing of either, but, through imitation, greatly impressing my religious contemporaries, much to my pleasure. It was on this 'campaign' that I met some 'Pentecostals' and since their arguments seemed, at that time, to agree with the Bible, I embraced their views and copied them. I indulged in such antics as yelling at the top of my voice in public prayer (though I rarely prayed in private), listening to people talking in 'tongues' (though I couldn't do it myself), having hands laid on my head, fasting publicly, watching a supposedly demon-afflicted man have a convulsion, and laying hands on a Ford Transit to 'exorcise the evil spirit out'.

This progress in religion helped only to make me more self-absorbed, superstitious and hypocritically proud than I had been before. I was made 'rather the worse'.

A change, however, was mercifully to come.

I had heard a preacher—John Metcalfe—and being reasonably impressed on one hearing agreed to hear him at a conference in Largs, Scotland, in October 1967, where he spoke on I John 2:28-3:3 over a series of three addresses. I was overwhelmed with the power with which Mr. Metcalfe spoke and was convicted by the standards which he seemed to expect of a true Christian, but managed to push it off by the supposition that other people there were more eligible for the searchings of the preaching that I heard.

Later, however, I began to realize that words and a profession were not enough, and that a real acquaintance with Christ, to know that he died for me, and to know his present living Person and his power in my soul were what was needed. The sandy foundations were increasingly eroded away until my house collapsed and I first doubted, and then was sure, that I had never been saved at all; that it was all unreal, and would only serve to make my hell worse.

A great distance from God, never realized in a religious profession, a love for sin, never admitted under comfortable preaching, and an inability to improve my state, never known amongst religious activities brought on a rebellion in my heart against God for being alive in such misery.

I knew I was going to hell, but didn't know how to get free. I began to discover a little of what my heart was like but I knew not how to change it—nor could I find help in books, though I looked into past ages, especially the Puritan era, to find it, since I was either encouraged to rest in Christ, which I didn't know how to do, or else was sent away with a sense of

God's anger and indignation against me for such daring disobedience. I became tangled up with such questions as, 'How do I believe?', 'What is it to come to Christ?', 'Am I elect?'

At times my heart sank in me, as I feared that I had sinned against the Holy Ghost and had never hope of mercy in this life or the next. At other times I hardened and tended towards being satisfied with my state and hence became slothful about my eternal salvation, being discouraged about the collapse of my previous religious profession.

I tried to induce a conversion experience such as I thought was necessary, thinking that somehow God would overshadow my soul and I would suddenly be made different. Several times I thought I was converted but, as often, it came to nothing and eventually I began to despair and became more miserable and self-pitying and, as a result, more rebellious and worldly.

I hated myself, was jealous of those who were converted, and blamed God in my heart for my state yet feared when I realised that I did.

Needless to say, my relations didn't know what to make of me nor how to help me. I and one or two friends who were more or less in the same sort of state, though we were little help to each other, found that our former religious connections were more or less broken since we were strange people to those who still held fast to those things which we found a positive burden.

I had resolved to hear Mr. Metcalfe preach again, and receiving an invitation from friends went to London to stay for a week under his preaching. The first meeting I went to, he said he felt no liberty to preach and so didn't. Since I felt it was because I was hardening my heart against being converted and since by the time the next meeting came I still felt unconverted, I didn't go to it fearing a repetition of the previous meeting.

Later, when I saw him, Mr. Metcalfe said two things to me personally which struck my soul. The first was, 'You know he died for you, don't you?' and the second was in prayer when he prayed that I would, 'deny thee no longer the heart that thou longest for'.

I didn't understand how these things could be since, as to the first, I had shut myself out of the Saviour's death by theological barriers of my own confused making and, as to the second, it was a strange thing to me that the Lord Jesus Christ should *want* my heart, and that he should want *my* heart.

I continued in a grey misery and an intellectual tangle until, despairing, broken, and utterly miserable, I went on my knees and pleaded for mercy because of the Lord Jesus Christ. For what was the first time in my life I felt a sense of peace and a sense that the Lord Jesus looked on me with compassion.

Through a belief that, after being converted, one was made perfect, and finding I wasn't, I soon doubted, but being encouraged by Psalm 103:8 'The Lord is gracious and merciful, slow to anger, and plenteous in mercy', I went again on my knees and found peace.

It was about April 1969, at a visit of Mr. Metcalfe's to the Tent Hall in Glasgow, when he preached on Isaiah 53:10,11, that I saw the value of the offering that Christ had made for the sins of his people in suffering for them and at that meeting I lifted my heart to God and made Christ's soul an offering, in a sensible appreciation that only this could appease God's righteous anger against my sins.

When I left school I moved to Tylers Green, where a church has been raised up by God under Mr. Metcalfe's ministry. I moved because I had heard nobody else who could preach the gospel of salvation experimentally in the Holy Ghost in such a way, and who could tell me more about the Lord Jesus Christ and his death in such clear doctrinal terms, nor could I find a group of people so in the power of salvation as these who were knit together in one under the sound of the gospel.

I was heartily received by minister and congregation and have been almost three years under the preaching of the gospel and in heart union with those who have found salvation and who love the Lord Jesus Christ.

Though I would have gone back and though I am so weak, yet, wonderfully, I have been kept and led in the truth. Under the preaching of the gospel I have found that God is Light and that those things lit up—treacherous ways, man pleasing ways, off-centre ulterior motives in religion, the 'secrets of men'—are not only lit up but dealt with, in spiritual exercise, in a way which was never so while I was in the dark.

While I realise that there is much I don't know, and more that I haven't experienced and so much of Canaan not yet trodden on, and so much of the world and its religion still in me, yet I am enabled, under the clear declaration of the truth, to lay my immortal soul more and more in trust upon the Lord Jesus Christ, who is the same yesterday, today and for ever. I am enabled to look away more and more to him who has swallowed up all the sufferings due to my sins, and all God's wrath against my person and state, to the one who, in his immense Person, has brought me that infinite distance to God and the Father by his precious, worthy blood.

Nigel Johnstone

The Conversion of
Jenny Smyth,
a fourteen-years-old schoolgirl

Miss Jenny Smyth,
Chalfont St. Peter,
Buckinghamshire.

I was brought up as a modernist, and, consequently, ever since I was about seven I had found myself unable to believe that there was a God. I was certain that the Bible had been made up to deceive us. Yet this was against my inmost sense. Because these thoughts terrified me, and I was certain that unbelief would damn me, I tried to push them to the back of my mind.

I was crying one night because I still could not believe, and was told that: 'Someone must have made us, so why not call that person God?' This made me feel much easier for a time.

The church services were no use to me: I just found them boring. At odd times I was able to believe that there was a God—in particular one night, when all my fears departed from me. One sermon I heard, the minister said he was speaking to those who could believe everything but the resurrection, and had come to give that a last trial. I knew that I could not believe anything, and hoped that what he said would help me, but went away as fearful as before.

As time went on I pushed my fears to the back of my mind, and wholeheartedly became a modernist as I had been led to believe. I was told that God never interfered in the world, and I began to wonder what he did do, and what the point of my religion really was. Paul describes my state: 'having the form of godliness but not the power thereof'.

I was troubled by my sinfulness, although I knew nothing of the wickedness of my nature. I seized many opportunities to try and make myself better. Each time I failed. When I was twelve, I determined that as soon as I was thirteen I would be better. Needless to say, I was not. Much of one holiday abroad with my parents, when I was thirteen, was spent in looking at the architecture of various Roman Catholic churches. When they were not looking I would go to the 'holy' water and make the sign of the cross on my forehead, hoping that that would make me clean, but it did not. I made myself a book saying all the things which I should do each day and how I should behave. I thought that if I kept to the book, as soon as I returned home, I would be much improved. I soon threw the book away.

The Roman Catholic idea of confession appealed to me, and as a substitute I wrote down all my faults in a book each day, hoping that this would stop me from repeating them. I soon stopped this.

Although I doubted what point my religion had, I knew no other, so continued in it. I was occasionally frightened out of my complacency by wondering what proof I had that there was a God.

The first time I went to the Meeting Hall at Tylers Green I was very sceptical, and ready to criticise everything which I heard. Although I rarely read the Bible I held the popular view that much of it was made up of legends. However, when Mr. Metcalfe went to prayer he particularly mentioned its inspiration, blessing God for it. As he said this, all my cynicism fell from me and I wanted to hear him preach.

The text was John 14:16-20 and I was struck by the nineteenth verse—'Yet a little while and the world seeth me no more, but ye see me.' The difference between the 'ye' who saw the Lord, and 'the world', which saw him not, was clearly shown. I had never heard of an experimental religion before, but knew that all I heard was the truth. I was convinced that I was a sinner, in need of salvation and longed to be of the 'ye'. Mr. Metcalfe said 'I am saved; are you?' I knew well that I was not, and that night I cried to the Lord that I might be.

The following week Mr. Metcalfe told me that he knew that I would be saved, which gave me great hope that I might be. I was worried that I would not recognise salvation when it came, having no idea what communion with the Lord was.

During the sermon the following day, on the same text as previously, I felt the Lord draw near to me and enter my heart. He had been so far from me, but I now felt his presence within me and his love filling me. I could truly see him in an inward way.

This did not go, but stayed with me. It was not a passing feeling, but continuous. I had no more trouble about believing that there was a God—I experienced that there was, and that he was willing to save sinners through his Son.

At that time I knew little of what had happened to me. I was like the blind man who had been given his sight, who said: 'One thing I know, that, whereas I was blind, now I see.' I could feel that he had entered my heart. He seemed to be *in* me and his love filled me. I realised that what had been said in the sermon was fulfilled in me. I had been of the world, but the Lord had made me one of the 'ye', who were of himself, and he had opened my inward eyes to see him.

Jenny Smyth

The Conversion of Jenny Smyth

Narrative note:

Jenny's parents' reaction to her joyful transformation at fourteen years old was not encouraging. They strictly prohibited her from going to any more meetings, forbidding her even the least contact with the saints at Tylers Green or with their children. This diktat was to run for two years. Ascribing everything to exterior influence—from but two meetings!—and nothing to interior power, the presumption was that after two years' isolation all Jenny's new religious fervour would wither and die, and her previous worldly 'normality' would return. If this had been, as was supposed, the influence of man, that conclusion might have been psychologically sound: but if it was the work of God, then who could overturn it, child of fourteen or not? The following letters were 'smuggled' out during the two years of strict isolation. When Jenny was sixteen she was reunited with the saints in Christ and to this day continues in the faith with them to worship the Father in spirit and in truth.

Jenny's letters, written between fourteen and sixteen years old, now follow:

Chalfont St. Peter,
Bucks.

8th June, 1970

Dear Mr. Metcalfe,

Greetings in the Lord Jesus.

On the surface there is not so much trouble at home now, so I can write to you without the risk of getting you into trouble.

On the Sunday when I returned from the music course, half a term ago, mummy told me her own version of what happened when she and daddy came to see you. She also added her opinions about you, which were not very nice ones. The day before we went back to school she asked me not to have much discussion with anyone from the Meeting, but apart from that nothing happened.

Since then nothing has occurred until recently. One biology lesson, a schoolgirl from the Meeting and I were told that we could not sit next to one another due to a notice which had been put up in the staff room by Miss Thurston the Headmistress. We thought that a mistake had been made so we took no notice until Mrs. Shutt told me on Friday that my parents had complained that the Meeting schoolgirls were dominating me.

I asked mummy about it on Friday night and she said that Miss Thurston had put the notice up and it was at the parents' evening that mummy and daddy complained. After a short argument I told mummy, when she asked what I thought she was, that I did not consider her a Christian. I had been wanting to say that for a long time because I thought that if they (mummy and daddy) died without me saying anything then it would be partly my fault that they went to hell because they thought they were Christians and I knew that they were not saved. Anyway, mummy said that I had no right to say that because only God knew whether we were Christians and I was setting myself up as God and judging her by saying it.

I read a text in Isaiah which said that our minds would be opened to know our own teachers, and I certainly know that she is not a teacher for me, but otherwise, was she right?

At the moment I am reading Huntington, for the second time, and I am reading Ephesians. Last R.E. lesson Mr. Clifford told us about the 'legend' of Jonah and he carefully explained how Jonah symbolised Israel. Jonah being swallowed by a fish symbolised the Jews being taken into exile! The previous lesson we had learnt about the 'legend' of Ruth, and that the story was based on an old folk tale. Thus it was not meant to be believed, for it was written as a protest against the commands of Ezra and Nehemiah! It is terrible to think how many people will have believed him.

Next year Mr. Clifford is going to America so we shall have a new R.E. teacher. When mummy saw Mr. Clifford at the parents' evening she said she thought he was very sincere and she liked him!

Today (Sunday) a preacher from Chalfont St. Giles took the service at mummy's church. He was really awful. In a children's talk he explained how shepherds used not to go to church because they were guarding their flock, and that God would know whether we came to church for his blessing, or whether we missed church either because we didn't want to go or because, like the shepherd, we couldn't go. Really, he made going to church sound a duty which, if you didn't obey, would get one into trouble. I suppose that is what some people at mummy's church would think because it is not possible to enjoy the service there.

I still go out to Junior church so I always miss the sermon. Daddy said that the minister took his text from John 17 and he proceeded to say that some churches were very extreme in separating themselves from the world while others were too worldly, so one should go half way between the two extremes. I am sure that daddy said this in order to point out that the Meeting, according to him, is like the first extreme; but how could he imagine that his church wasn't at the other extreme in being worldly? Not that in comparison with most other churches it is especially worldly—they all seem to be as bad as each other.

Last Sunday one of the boys tried to explain that Adam and Eve showed the principles of evolution, and this week he said that Jesus was the first communist!

There is no hope that mummy and daddy will let me come to the Meeting before I am sixteen. Two years seems an awfully long way away and I am praying that, if it is God's will, I might come to the Meeting soon—it is sometimes difficult to even remember what a true church is like. When I first came home I found it difficult to believe that mummy and daddy would keep me away from the Meeting but they are not nearly so tolerant as I once thought! I fear that when I become sixteen they may go back on what they have said. Meanwhile, although I can't see you I can at least write as much as possible.

With my love to you all,

from Jenny

From John Metcalfe
Tylers Green,
Penn,
Bucks.

Tuesday A.M.

My Dear Daughter in the faith,

Grace to you, mercy and peace, from God our Father and the Lord Jesus Christ.

Your letter gave me very great pleasure, and I want you to know how delighted I am to hear from you. I felt within myself the movings of the love of God for your soul, which spring out of everlasting eternity from the bowels of sovereign compassion, and which love is free, unmerited, and rejoices over us with unutterable tenderness, and will not suffer our foot to be moved, but will preserve us from all evil.

This love brings in a free righteousness through his blood, it breaks the bands of death, dismisses the gloom of the grave, and brings us, with joy unspeakable and full of glory, into his eternal inheritance.

I was enabled to pray for you in the Spirit, and felt strong consolation that my dear daughter has been kept by the power of God, maintained by his indwelling Spirit, that her love to her Lord Jesus, who manifests himself to her—but not the world, which sees him no more—I say, her love to this her sweet Saviour is fresh, fervent, watered by the dews of heaven, and kept in the knowledge of the truth by prayer and the reading of the word.

Truly I can say, the bonds of spiritual affection begotten in the Holy Ghost, are stronger than fleshly ties! For I remember you in secret before God and the Father, as in a love not begotten by parentage in birth, but in God out of eternity, and feeling this, you have never been out of my mind. But I do praise God to hear from you, and know that your soul prospers.

Remember my dear, the awful lessons of God's law: the total depravity of man, the utter bondage of will; the corruption and rottenness of the flesh; the worthlessness of the natural heart, which is deceitful above all things and desperately wicked—who can know it? Jer. 17:9. Moreover the rebellious enmity of the carnal intellect, Rom. 8. Again, the blasphemy of dead works, the whitewash of daubing the dead sepulchre of self-righteousness with the form of religion; that God loathes this hypocrisy, and accepts none of it, but is utterly removed in his holiness from all that the flesh presumptuously thrusts towards him and calls worship. Finally, the terrors of his wrath. This is revealed against all ungodliness and unrighteousness of men, and is a revelation from heaven. The law condemns the whole world, shutting every mouth, none excepted, Rom. 3:19, and closes the door of death on every soul who by works sought to justify themselves by religion or without it, to the torments of that hell in which their worm never dieth, their fire is not quenched, and on which the Saviour himself has informed us, the wrath of God abides.

But blessed be God for his free grace to poor lost sinners! Oh how sweet a saving view of the wonderful Lord Jesus. Oh how soul melting the inward peace from the Spirit's application of his all-atoning blood! How glorious to know the grace that meets the sinner, as lost and dead, freely clothes him with a righteous robe of justification by faith only, gives him remission of sins, ransom of soul, redemption of person, gives him the faith of God's elect and, by regeneration in the Holy Ghost, sets the saints apart for his holy service.

May God bless these few words in love to your soul. Keep close accounts with God; keep a clear conscience. No man has the right to make you do wrong, especially in worship. When you feel able and old enough, no longer tolerate men's oppression, but fear God! And whatsoever your lovely Saviour, Jesus, saith unto you, that do.

Grace be with you, my dear; and my prayers follow you in love.

Yours eternally,
John Metcalfe

Chalfont St. Peter,
Bucks.

16th July, 1970

Dear Mr. Metcalfe,

Greetings in the love of God, the everlasting Father, and in our dear Redeemer. Thank you very much for your letter. The Lord has blessed it to me, and I want you to know how delighted I was to hear from you.

I am reading Madame Guyon at the moment, and indeed I can say with her how good God has been to me, and with what ingratitude I have repaid him.

I used to complain within myself that I could not go to any meetings, and that I could see no Christians apart from sometimes at school, and when I was with them Miss Thurston tried to separate us. How could I complain! God has indeed been merciful unto me through the dear Lord Jesus and on one Lord's day I felt as though his love was shining into my heart. Yet, instead of praising and glorifying his name I immediately went away from him. I had always tried to get up early, so that I might pray to him, but although I had read of Huntington's experience I still began to cry, 'A little more sleep, a little more slumber, a little more folding of the hands to sleep'; and poverty did come as one that travelleth, and my want was that of an armed man.

Yet God has ever been with me, unfaithful as I am, and when I read your letter I discovered that I had truly been taught of God. How great is our God! His kindness is unfailing, even to one as vile and undeserving as me. I can only praise and thank him for his goodness to an unworthy worm and I can only praise the Lord for my salvation.

When we were given our R.E. exam papers back I found that where I had mentioned the doctrine of predestination it was underlined plus five large question marks and an even larger exclamation mark. On asking him why this was so, Mr. Clifford, the R.E. teacher, replied that predestination was a 'silly idea'. And when he heard that I thought that man had no free choice whether he could be saved or not, Mr. Clifford looked at me as though I was half-witted. Incidentally, Madame Guyon also says that man has free choice, whether to accept or resist grace. This isn't right is it? For surely man has nothing to do with his salvation.

There was a different preacher at mummy's church on Sunday who was worse than the usual one. In every prayer he was very disrespectful to our God, saying you instead of thee so I was not joining in the prayer. Thus I noticed that the minister could not close his eyes in prayer, because he had to keep looking down at his notes to check that he was saying the right thing and to find out what he had to say next. The text of his sermon was a Hippy theme 'doing your thing', which he linked up with the Bible. He said that if the ear did the eye's work we could not hear, and thus every man should do his own thing and not anyone else's. No doubt this is why Paul says: 'Look not every man on his own things, but every man also on the things of others'!

Indeed that preacher and Mr. Clifford do seem to be blind guides, and greedy dogs or shepherds that cannot understand.

On Friday we break up and there will be nearly seven weeks without me seeing a Christian. I will ring up as much as possible, and I trust in the Lord Jesus that I may soon see you and that I may go to a meeting.

With love and affection in the Lord Jesus,

Jenny

Chalfont St. Peter,
Bucks.

10th January, 1971

Dear Mr. Metcalfe,

Greetings in the name of the ever lovely Jesus, who died for us while we were yet sinners, that we might be saved.

How great is our God. His mercy and lovingkindness to us is wonderful. That the God of Abraham and David is our God!

Time and again we grieve him, and break his commandments. I am sure that there has never been such a sinner as me, yet his dear love is unchanging. Indeed we can cry with Paul, 'Oh the depth of the riches both of the wisdom and knowledge of God. How unsearchable are his judgments, and his ways past finding out', Romans 11:33. For by his grace I was saved, by grace I have been kept from falling into hell, and I trust that his grace will keep me to the last. His grace will ever be sufficient.

It is nearly a year since my salvation, and it is a constant source of wonder to me how God has kept such a sinful and rebellious worm from falling into hell. How many times have I despised, 'the riches of his goodness and forbearance and longsuffering', Romans 2:4. I am indeed a witness that it is by the grace of God alone that I am what I am.

How terrible is God's wrath against the ungodly. For, 'the smoke of their torment ascendeth up for ever and ever: and they have no rest day nor night, who worship the beast and his image, and whosoever receiveth the mark of his name', Rev. 14:11. Such death is the wages of sin, but blessed be our

God who has given us the gift of eternal life through Christ Jesus our Lord, 'who has washed us from our sins in his own blood and hath made us kings and priests unto God and his Father; to him be glory and dominion for ever and ever', Rev. 1:5.

How glorious is our Saviour who washed us in his dear, redeeming blood. What agony did he endure on the cross, that he might save all his sheep from the curse of the law; all the suffering of the elect was compressed into three hours. Indeed the death of our bleeding Saviour is the essence of Christianity—what love did he show towards us, 'For scarcely for a righteous man will one die: yet peradventure for a good man some would even dare to die. But God commendeth his love toward us, in that, while we were yet sinners, Christ died for us', Romans 5:7,8. Our sins were as scarlet and he made them as white as snow; though they were red like crimson, he made them as white as wool (Isaiah 1:18) and again, 'He was wounded for *our* transgressions, he was bruised for *our* iniquities: the chastisement of *our* peace was upon him; and with his stripes we are healed', Isaiah 53:5.

The world cannot see the Lord any more because they walk 'in the vanity of their minds, having the understanding darkened, being alienated from the life of God through the ignorance that is in them because of the blindness of their heart', Ephesians 4:17,18. But Jesus has said unto us, 'Yet a little while, and the world seeth me no more; but ye see me: because I live ye shall live also', John 14:19. How wonderful is salvation, which has given us eyes to see, shown us light and brought us to God. We shall ever have cause to bless and praise his dear name.

With love in the Lord Jesus,

Jenny

Chalfont St. Peter,
Bucks.

6th March, 1971

Dear Mr. Metcalfe,

Greetings in the name of the Lord Jesus Christ, who has saved us from the wrath of God by washing us from our sins in his own blood.

Thank you very much for the book 'More than Notion' which you gave me for my birthday. I have found it much easier to understand the difference between formal religion and experimental religion, after reading some of it. There are many wonderful accounts of the Lord's dealings with his people in it. Reading this has lead me to reflect upon my own conversion, and how great God has been to one so unworthy.

How great is our God. How wonderful are his mercies to us. We were deep in the way of sin when he called us unto him, away from darkness into light. Before his salvation we were filled with unrighteousness. Puffed up with vanity and self-pride, committing all manner of evil and breaking his commandments. We were directly opposed to the way of God. How wonderful is his love that he brought us out of our awful state, by sending his Son to redeem the elect.

Redemption through the blood of Jesus is too wonderful for us to fully comprehend. What love Jesus had towards us, to suffer so. His salvation is so unmerited. Jesus died for us while we were yet sinners. He gave his life for polluted worms who grieved him continuously. All our guilt is washed away in his dear blood. He meets all the sinner's needs. He covers our nakedness with a robe of righteousness. He opens the eyes of our understanding. We were wretched, miserable and poor. He made us rich in his love and joyous in his salvation. We were lost, and he gave us a finished salvation. Such truths as these can never be discussed or reflected on enough. Blessed be our precious Jesus!

Those who are unconverted, and die so, will be subject to the wrath of God. The great debt, which all mankind owed God, and has been paid for the elect by Jesus, will be required of them. They will be raised from the dead in the same body with which they have lusted and sinned against God. Only then will we realise the true greatness of our salvation.

Even as infinity in this world reflects a little of the greatness of God, eternity will do likewise in the next. We, who are used to a repetitive span of days, weeks, months and years cannot visualise eternity. Before time began God loved us and sanctified us. When time ends we will still abide in the love of God. 'Nor height, nor depth, nor any other creature, shall be able to separate us from the love of God, which is in Christ Jesus our Lord', Romans 8:39.

The Holy Spirit, who convicted us of sin before our salvation, will bring us safely to the day of the Lord Jesus. What a wonderful time that will be, when the Lord avenges himself upon all his enemies, who seem to have control of the world at present. To unbelievers the thought of the last judgment should present terror, but the language of our hearts should be the same as John's: 'Even so, come Lord Jesus.'

With love and affection in the Lord Jesus,

Jenny

Chalfont St. Peter,
Bucks.

2nd April, 1971

Dear Mr. Metcalfe,

Greetings in the name of our glorious Redeemer, who has suffered and died for us that our sins might be blotted out and that we might be reconciled unto God.

How wonderful is our Redeemer. That he should show his love to those who are so unworthy. He knows that we are but dust. He knows our polluted natures and the depth of our dark, sinful hearts—yet still he loves us. That he, who is so lovely, should appear to those who are so vile. We have despised and rejected him. Our sins pierced his hands and feet. Our ungodliness wounded his side, but he has shone his light into our hearts. He has clothed us, and washed us in his own blood. He had saved us from the torment of hell, and brought us unto God. Blessed Jesus! We will ever have cause to praise his dear name.

It is wonderful to know that Christ Jesus is our 'all in all'. How many times we experience that without him we can do nothing. If we were left to ourselves, how soon we should fall. All praise and glory to God for his grace, which alone keeps our feet from falling and our steps from slipping. We know that we can attribute nothing to ourselves because we are nothing but sin and weakness. All glory must be given to our God—for 'the foolishness of God is wiser than men; and the weakness of God is stronger than men', I Cor. 1:25. What love and mercy has he shown towards us, and with what sin and base ingratitude have we repaid him. Our ways are contrary to his and our flesh rebels against all that is godly. That he can accomplish good through such awful instruments —yet he can, and he has; for with him, nothing is impossible.

How wonderful is our God. 'He is righteous in all his ways, and holy in all his works', Psalm 145:17. He has shown us the secret which was hidden to our forefathers—his own love in Jesus Christ. We know that 'the secret of the Lord is with them that fear him', Psalm 25:14. However, this fear does not come from any godliness in us, but it is implanted by God. As it is written, 'I will put my fear in their hearts, that they shall not depart from me', Jeremiah 32:40. We are compelled to say with Peter, that we are 'kept by the grace of God unto salvation', nothing is from ourselves.

When our Redeemer shows us his love and how he suffered for us, we can only fall at his feet, and worship him, like the two Marys did when he rose from the dead. We can cry with those in the book of Revelation 'Worthy is the Lamb that was slain ... Blessing and honour, and glory and power, be unto him that sitteth upon the throne, and unto the Lamb for ever and ever', Revelation 5:12,13.

With love and affection in the Lord Jesus,

Jenny

Chalfont St. Peter,
Bucks.

27th June, 1971

Dear Mr. Metcalfe,

Greetings in the name of our sweet Saviour, Jesus, who has redeemed us by his own blood, and ever lives to make intercession for us, Heb. 7:25.

How wonderful are our Father's dealings with his children. When he hides his face from us, it is for our own good. That he should bear with those who are so vile and unworthy of the least of his mercies. When thinking of his dealings with us, we can remember how he called us, when we were not seeking him but running from him, and sinning against him. What love he showed towards us when he chose us to be saved—not for any merit of our own, but as is his blessed will. For 'God hath chosen the foolish things of the world to confound the wise; and God hath chosen the weak things of the world to confound the things which are mighty; and base things of the world, and things which are despised, hath God chosen, yea, and things which are not, to bring to naught things that are: that no flesh should glory in his presence', I Cor. 1:27-29. We know our sinful nature well enough to realise that if there was any way in which we could praise ourselves for our salvation we would do so, but God has so ordained it that salvation should be all of him, and not of us. We play a merely passive part. We are not free to resist grace —if it was so, none of us would ever have been saved since the Spirit and the flesh are so contrary to one another, Gal. 5:17. Jesus says 'Ye have not chosen me, but I have chosen you, and ordained you, that ye should go and bring forth fruit', John 15:16.

What love has God shown towards us, who are so unworthy. We know that we would wander from him if we were left to ourselves, but how many times have we found him 'a very present help in trouble', Psalm 46:1. What reason we have to cry the song of Moses, and of the Lamb, 'Great and marvellous are thy works, Lord God Almighty; just and true are thy ways, thou King of saints', Rev. 15:3.

Blessed Jesus! Sweet Saviour! How wonderful is his indwelling presence, how sweet is communion with him—that we can speak with him! He has promised that he will never leave us, or forsake us, and that he will ever be with us. What security is this! Indeed, nothing can separate us from the love of our Jesus. Paul says that 'neither death, nor life, nor angels, nor principalities, nor powers, nor things present, nor things to come, nor height, nor depth, nor any other creature, shall be able to separate us from the love of God, which is in Christ Jesus our Lord', Rom. 8:38,39.

Christ has bidden us to watch for the day of his coming. How wonderful will that day be! The language of our hearts is the same as that of John—'Quickly come Lord Jesus.'

With love in the dear Lord Jesus,

Jenny

Chalfont St. Peter,
Bucks.

26th October, 1971

Dear Mr. Metcalfe,

Greetings in the name of the Lord Jesus Christ. I should like to share with you some of the wondrous dealings of God with my soul. Truly, the way in which he keeps his children is wonderful. We have all experienced that we are poor, lost sinners who can do nothing without him. He alone can preserve us from the many snares and pitfalls which are around us. Peter says that we are 'kept by the power of God through faith unto salvation ready to by revealed in the last time', I Peter 1:5.

You have probably heard that I was abroad for five weeks with my parents in the summer holidays. You can imagine that the lack of privacy in the caravan worried me considerably before I went on the holiday. I continually experience how dead I am unless I have time alone with God each morning. However, I was kept throughout the five weeks in the most wonderful way. A lot of the time was spent travelling, and on some journeys my Redeemer's presence was very sweet. I think that it is true that each day I was taught something new.

I had been feeling for some time that it was wrong for me to continue to attend my parents' church. Last Sunday I told mummy that I did not wish to go any more. How blessed is our God—instead of the numerous arguments which I had been expecting, he had been leading her thoughts in the same way as mine. She and daddy had realised that the service meant nothing to me, and did not benefit me in any way, and had already agreed that there was no sense in me continuing to go. They would like me to go for the remaining weeks of their minister's ministry (he is retiring in about three weeks' time).

I cannot praise my God enough for the wonderful way in which I have been kept, since my salvation. When I first was saved, two years seemed a dreadfully long time to be without the meetings—yet now, God willing, there are only four or five months left. My birthday is towards the end of February, and that is the time when my parents have said that I can go.

Looking back over God's dealings with us is very humbling. To see how he loved us, and was leading us, even when we were dead in our sins and were running from him. His past love to us in calling us, his present love in keeping us and watching over us, and his future love, when we will be with him, and the flesh shall not separate us from him any more. Truly, the love in appointing Jesus to be our Saviour, in bruising his own Son that we might be justified, is too great for our meagre comprehension. None of us can pretend to understand one thousandth of God's greatness, his justice, his wrath, or his love. 'Oh the depth of the riches both of the wisdom and knowledge of God! how unsearchable are his judgments, and his ways past finding out!', Rom. 11:33.

The love of Jesus, the atonement which he made for our sins, his faith which justifies us—all is too great for us to understand. He was hanging on the cross for us. Our sins were the nails which pierced him—we cannot claim to have done anything worthy of eternal life, all we have done is to pierce our sweet Saviour and to break the law from which we are now redeemed.

Blessed is our Jesus that we *are* now redeemed. We are not now walking in the vanity of our minds, being alienated from the life of God through the ignorance which is in us, Eph. 4:17,18. We have been called to holiness, not uncleanliness (I Thess. 4:7) and must now live to serve and praise our God and the Lord Jesus, who has done so much for us. Each one of us, I am sure, wishes his life to be superior to what it is. Oh for a life ever filled with the love of Christ, a life dedicated to our Creator!

What power is shown to us by the creation—all see and admire the work of God's hands, yet few look through creation to the Creator, and realise that soon all shall see the power and justice of God. God alone can awaken man to see that only time keeps him from paying for all his sins in hell. Only God can show us that Jesus has taken away the sins of his people, and their eternity will not be one of torments but one of perfect joy.

With love in our dear Redeemer's name,

Jenny

74

Chalfont St. Peter,
Bucks.

16th January, 1972

Dear Mr. Metcalfe,

Greetings in the love of God our Father, who keeps us from falling by his grace alone, and is ever watching over us.

The way in which God keeps his children will always be a constant source of amazement to us. Not one of us can say that we have done anything at all that is right—without him we would be completely lost.

If we consider how great God is—too great for our feeble minds to comprehend, we can only be astonished that he should care for us at all, let alone make us his children. We are all so vile, and so utterly unworthy of all his mercies to us. Our hearts turned away from God. We did not desire any knowledge of him. 'The heart is deceitful above all things, and desperately wicked: who can know it?', Jer. 17:9.

Even while we were turning against God, and sinning against him, he loved us in Jesus. He called us even while we were dishonouring him—for none of us have come to God unsought, nor could we do so. Of ourselves, we would never choose the right way.

Christ died for us, 'while we were yet sinners'. We had done nothing for him—we were justly under the wrath of God due to our many transgressions—yet all our sins were punished in Jesus. What wonderful love this was. His blood has completely cleansed us. He has done all, we have done nothing.

Not only were we reconciled to God by Christ's death, but we were saved when God raised him from the dead, Romans

5:10. His conduct towards us has been so loving, and so merciful; and we have repaid him with sin and ingratitude in return. We are worms, frail creatures made from dust, yet God calls us his children. 'Behold, what manner of love the Father hath bestowed upon us, that we should be called the sons of God', I John 3:1.

Even though God has done so much for us, we still do not love him, or serve him, as we should. I can only feel ashamed that I am so ungrateful, and that my life is so unholy. Whenever I wander away from him, he welcomes me back with such love that I feel ashamed, and am certain that I will not go against him again, yet shortly, the same thing happens. I make resolutions only to break them, and can only say with Paul, 'For I know that in me (that is, in my flesh) dwelleth no good thing: for to will is present with me; but how to perform that which is good I find not, for the good that I would I do not: but the evil which I would not, that I do', Rom. 7:18,19.

When I look over the time which God has been with me, I can only marvel at his patience and goodness towards me. I am far removed from what I should be. That God should love me at all is past my understanding, but that he should guide me and teach me, as he has, is truly wonderful.

It is nearly two years since I have seen you, and I can only thank God that he has kept me through that time. Soon, I trust, I shall be able to see you again. As you know my parents have said that I may go to the Meeting when I am sixteen, and my sixteenth birthday is on February 24th. I am longing for that time, as you can imagine.

God has given our lives some purpose, we have something to live for—that we may be used for his glory. That he can be glorified in such vile things as ourselves is remarkable—yet he can, and he will be. What a wonderful salvation, that gives all the glory to him, in which we ourselves do nothing. Even though we are such sinners, still we try and secure glory to ourselves, and are puffed up with vain self-pride, and conceit.

How often we readily make time for worldly things, and forget about the things of God. How often our minds are taken up with things that do not matter. Reading the Bible should be our chief pleasure—yet how often it becomes a burden and a painful duty, or gets neglected completely. Sometimes days pass when I scarcely think of God at all—how wrong this is, yet how often it happens.

This would not happen if Jesus was always before us, but how often we take our eyes from him, and then we fall. How lovely is our Saviour. His sufferings for us were so great. We ourselves pierced his hands and his feet with our sins. Our ungodliness was the crown of thorns which was put on his head. From this we know that what Paul says applies to us too, when he says: 'Christ loved me, and gave himself for me.' What love this was, that washed us clean from all our sins. 'Unto him that loved us, and washed us from our sins in his own blood, and hath made us kings and priests unto God and his Father; to him be glory and dominion for ever and ever', Rev. 1:5,6.

How precious is his love to us during every day. When he is shining into our hearts, what joy we feel, what happiness, but when he is gone, how hard and cold we feel. When he is with us, we can only fall at his feet and thank him for all he has done, but when we lose his presence, how quickly our thoughts turn away from him.

We do not know what each day will bring. It is comforting to be able to trust in God that he will be with us, begging him to keep us safe 'unto the day of Christ Jesus'.

With much love in our Saviour,

Jenny

The Conversion of
Ian Kemp

IAN KEMP, a young man from Glasgow, was in rebellion against God and the gospel. To his great anger he heard his newly converted brother playing the tapes of Mr. Metcalfe's preaching in his bedroom. At first he would go to great lengths to avoid the sound. But he could not shut his ears, and, despite himself, began to listen intently. First shut up under the law to sin, 'My last letter was so full of lamentations over dry bones', afterwards he was brought into glorious gospel liberty through salvation in Christ.

From Ian Kemp

Dear Mr. Metcalfe,

My last letter was so full of lamentations over dry bones, but now I write to tell you of the wondrous joy in my heart ever since I knew I was converted. From that Tuesday night everything seems to have taken on a new light. My prayers, far from being dead, are times of great blessing and I never seem to be able to praise the Lord enough for his wondrous works. When I think of the stinking mess I was in when I was of the world, and how I dived into it as far as I possibly could, the mercy of God seems overwhelming and the work on the cross too wonderful for words.

As for Bible reading it seems as though I was reading some other book before because I now can see behind the words which are written. I used to diligently look up each reference

78

in the margin in a vain attempt to get something from my readings, but now the words seem to be so clear as to what they convey and not as they appear. For the first time I see the spiritual significances behind the passages. I don't know much doctrine yet but the knowledge of the blessed and wondrous work done for me is enough for the present.

It's a great honour now to sing the psalms of praise because I can sing them in honesty.

I'm sorry the letter is brief but the joy inside of me cannot be expressed on paper no matter how much I try.

Yours in the Lord,

Ian

The Conversion of Margaret Kendall

Hazlemere,
Bucks.
31st May, 1985

Dear Mr. Metcalfe,

This is an account of my experience as you requested.

My parents attended the Baptist church. I was sent to Sunday school and sometimes to 'church' but really we lived in a completely worldly way, without regard to God.

When I was fourteen years old I went with a party from the Baptist church to a 'Billy Graham' meeting at Harringay. The preaching had no effect on me and I could not remember, even shortly afterwards, what he preached about. However, during the appeal I felt I should 'give in' and decide to become a Christian. I told a friend and my mother the same evening that I wanted to be baptized, but I had no heartbrokenness for sin that I should desire a Saviour. I knew nothing of total depravity nor of justifying righteousness. I had no idea of the holiness or greatness of God or of my inability to approach him. I did not repent towards God and I had no appreciation of Christ at all. Yet, I thought I was a Christian and reformed my life in outward ways. I felt as if I was 'walking on air', but that joy was deceptive, as in the parable of the sower, where the seed was sown in that shallow ground which 'anon with joy receiveth it'.

I was accepted as a Christian by the Baptist church and was baptized, but I was not converted. I was totally presumptuous, proud in free will and devoid of any experience of law or gospel. Yet I could never settle in the Baptist church.

When I was seventeen I was invited to hear you preach at Hayes Town Chapel. I felt very strongly that I should go and when I heard this preaching I believed it was very much of God. Before long I severed my connections with West Ealing Baptist Church and came under your ministry. You were expounding Romans. You impressed on us that men must first have a Spirit given knowledge of sin and of judgment, if they are to be justified. I could see how right and reasonable that was, but it cut the ground from under my feet because I had had no such experience. You exhorted us, if we were in such a case, to start again, but I did not do this. I looked at the changes I had made and was blind to the false foundation, itself grounded in the sand of my deceitful free will. I tried hard to 'have faith', but unsurprisingly was easily moved. I was completely unstable and continued so for years, this being my own fault entirely.

The faithful preaching and reading of the scripture brought a knowledge of myself that I did not have before. I was convicted of sins that I had committed, particularly telling lies. The scriptures pricked me over this, e.g. Ananias and Sapphira in Acts 5, 'whosoever loveth and maketh a lie' in Rev. 22, and the passage in John 8 which speaks of the devil as a 'liar, and the father of it'.

You exhorted us to keep short accounts, but I would not put things right. I was convicted of not coming to the light, of walking in darkness. I did not like reading of the godly repentance of the Corinthians.

My sins were a great barrier between the Lord and me and they became an increasing burden to me but I *would not* deal with them. This brought home to me how that, at the bottom, my will was in total opposition to God.

I saw what a state of rebellion I was in because I would not submit to him over putting things right and I couldn't say 'Lord' because he was not Lord over everything in my life.

I avoided speaking of the Lord to people. The text 'Whosoever shall deny me before men, him will I also deny before my Father which is in heaven' worried me.

Alongside these convictions I had an increasing desire to experience God's dealings and to really be brought to him, but I knew it would have to be his work because I couldn't change my heart. It was 'deceitful' and 'desperately wicked'. I prayed that if it was possible he would change me, but I had almost given up hope of being any different.

Then in March of this year, 1985, you telephoned me following the sisters' prayer meeting on a Friday evening. You said I was dead and I knew you were right. You said that the Lord was moving amongst us. I knew I ought to submit to him and not resist. You also entreated me, 'Pray personally'. I had not prayed like that before others because it would have revealed what a dreadful state I was in.

I was in a turmoil that night and the next day. I was as unwilling as ever to deal with those sins, but, late in the afternoon, for no reason in myself, I cleared many of the things that had troubled me for so long, and that evening I did pray personally. I confessed the lies and the guile with which I had covered up so much. I knew what a deceitful heart I had. I was reduced to nothing—utterly destitute— unable to save myself. I was guilty. I deserved wrath. My only hope was in Christ as my substitute, dying for my sins and my sin. Passages of scripture came to me that I could plead—'I came not to call the righteous, but sinners to repentance'. 'To this man will I look, to him that is poor and of a contrite spirit' that 'trembleth at my word.' 'Whosoever shall call upon the name of the Lord shall be saved.' 'Him that cometh to me I will in no wise cast out.'

Certainly now at last I had a broken and a contrite heart and I believe that in mercy God heard me and gave me to appreciate the death of Christ in a way never experienced before.

He changed my heart from a stony to a fleshy heart. I really wanted to serve him—not sin; and I did come to the light and deal with the things that had been such a hindrance to me. I had a great desire to pray. I found I could say 'My Lord and my God', which I had not been able to before. I desired to read the scriptures, sing the Psalms and Songs and looked forward to meeting with the saints. I felt my captivity was turned into joy and liberty, and that the Lord had saved my soul and brought me to himself, not in 1954, but now, in 1985.

I am very grateful to you, Mr. Metcalfe, for preaching so faithfully and for applying the word to me and for not being satisfied with less than a true work. I bless God that you telephoned me on that Friday and would like to record that it was not your fault that I remained unsaved for so long a time.

With love in the Lord Jesus Christ,

Margaret Kendall

Margaret Kendall, a housewife,
is the mother of nine children.

The Conversion of
Elisabeth Barker

Castlefield,
Bucks.

3rd March, 1986

Dear Sirs,

If I go back as far as I can remember, I always hated life. I was a rebellious child, a rotten teenager, a failure as a mother, and a battered and abused wife. How could I expect Jesus Christ to save me?

I joined an Anglican church and gave the fragments of my soiled life to the Lord and was told I was saved.

What an empty, light, professing Christian I was. Until, to my distress, I started to sense the pretence, to experience the backbiting, and slowly and painfully realise the truth wasn't anywhere to be found there. And not only that, I was slowly starving to death.

I sneaked about among the members seeking relief but instead I found contempt and suspicion, many hands were laid on me, many prayers were prayed for me, and many 'demons' were cast out of me. In fact, I became like a zombie, I couldn't feel, I couldn't bear anyone to touch me. Jesus Christ, as I thought I knew him, was gone, and I had to live in a sort of nightmare with the most terrible depths of groanings coming from within. People dropped in, visited me, and I continued attending services but hated the emptiness of it all.

One day I just upped and left. I never went back, and relief and a certain joy started to flood in.

There were the usual things said, the usual difficult phone conversations, many tears of pain but also a deeper peace than I had known before. At least I had departed from the apostasy.

I still continued to try and work out the truth by reading many books, although in a very numb state. One day I walked into W.H. Smith's in High Wycombe and went to the Christian books. I picked up a book written by a Mr. Metcalfe. I was starving; no one will ever know the joy and comfort I felt in reading this book. At last, hope!

Could this really be? Yes, hope; I went back and bought 'The Messiah'. All I wanted to do was read, every spare moment. When my daughter, Natalie, didn't need me, I read; as soon as she went to bed, I read; as soon as she went to school, I read. I wept, I read and prayed.

On one occasion last year I sent to the Publishing Trust for two of Mr. Metcalfe's books, and, later, at the end of last year,

I received a calendar; I just had to phone and say thank you. This eventually led to a conversation with Mr. John Darroch, and it followed that I attended a meeting. Again such joy, and certainty, at last, a real worshipping people. And such truth. I began to realise the depth of my poverty of spirit, and the state of unbelief that I was in, but all this was spoken of, nothing hidden. How I've longed for faith to believe, living faith, saving faith.

At last I heard Mr. Metcalfe preach. It was on Sunday last, from Mark 16, and slowly light began to dawn on me, and I felt that I believed indeed. And if I do not believe the gospel which I heard preached that night, then there is nothing for me, because each and every one of my waking hours is dependent on the truth of Christ made known in the gospel. Therefore how could I possibly continue in unbelief? I know now, despite many doubtings, that Christ Jesus has been revealed to me as my only hope, and my salvation.

Elisabeth Barker

The Conversion of
Stephen Luford

High Wycombe,
Bucks.
19th July, 1989

The following is an account of my experience of God's dealings.

Being brought up in an ungodly family I lived without serious thought until my early twenties. When a restlessness started to be felt within, this started me seeking for something although I didn't know what, and, living in Australia at the time, my parents having emigrated when I was nine years old, I decided to visit England, having great imaginings of seeing Europe. Yet such was the beginning of my inward distress, that I stayed six months, spending almost the whole time in the front room of my aunt and uncle's Yorkshire council house watching T.V., returning home a failure. The following year I did the same.

Two years later, with my brother, I came again, this time visiting France, Belgium, Holland and England. Whilst we were in London our parents and youngest brother left Australia for good to come and live in England. Although I knew this was planned, I wasn't happy because I hated Europe and wanted to return to Australia.

Now I felt lost, all sense of belonging dissipated. Strange disturbance moved my soul; as I now know, this was the beginning of God's work in me. My parents settled in Bournemouth, we joined them; it was 1978. Within months, restless and tried, I decided to return to Australia. I said goodbye at the railway station, went up to Heathrow and was somehow stopped from my intention by a deep constraint. I stood staring at the check-in desk. I couldn't go. Moved from within, I returned to Bournemouth late at night. I couldn't face my parents, I sat in a park feeling totally dejected. Torn and even more restless, as if tossed by every wave, within weeks I returned to Australia with my brother; eight months later I was back in England.

It was during this period that I bought a bible, after having read a paperback called 'The Life of Jesus Christ', and although I had no understanding, I kept it and began to read Christian books, mostly rubbish written by men who, like myself, had no understanding.

The first I heard of Mr. Metcalfe was through my brother who, similarly awakened, told me how this man had said in one of his books that Moses stood for the law and after he died Joshua, who stood for the grace of Christ, led the people into the promised land. All this was a figure of obtaining rest in Christ. I was stunned by what I read. I had never heard it on this wise before. I began to read the books of Mr. Metcalfe and of others such as Bunyan and Luther, which, although they taught me that I wasn't saved, did not awaken me to my danger. I was still blinded by Satan about judgment and the wrath to come. I was very much in the world at this time, I'd moved into a flat in Bournemouth and surrounded myself with distractions. I didn't attend any of the 'churches' on a regular basis but, through a workmate, I did visit a Baptist 'Church', but I didn't like it, the people were very nice, too nice, and for some reason the focal point of the building was a small tiled swimming pool. So I stayed very much a loner, watching T.V. far more than reading the bible or the books of godly men.

The turning point for me was my awakening by the Holy Ghost in 1988, when I heard a tape of Mr. Metcalfe preaching, (Rom. 1:18-20) 'God revealed in Creation'. I heard the tape all the way through seemingly unaffected, and I was about to say to my brother, who had brought the tape, 'I will hear him again on this matter', when my brother suddenly burst into tears and said 'What's going to happen?' Such fear came upon me as I'd never felt before in my life; suddenly I looked out at the sky and I could sense the wrath to come. I heard the tape two or three times again, and I was reduced to tears at my folly.

A couple of weeks later in conversation my brother, equally convicted of sin and judgment, said, 'When we are lowered into the lake of fire', and, again, fear struck me with such force that I trembled. Days later I was alone listening to another tape in which Mr. Metcalfe described what eternal damnation would be like. I began to tremble and felt such guilt, knowing that as I stood I was going to be damned for my sin, and that death was no escape.

Everything had now changed and I tried to live a godly life, especially by copying the saints who I'd met on a visit to Tylers Green with my brother. Indeed, I desired the Lord in his mercy to bring me under Mr. Metcalfe's ministry. But now everything I did convicted me. At work I'd be halfway through my lunch when I'd realise I hadn't given thanks and be so convicted I couldn't eat another bite. My workmates, knowing nothing of my experience, still treated me as one of the lads, and I would go along with them and then be convicted, and other such like instances, until one evening, finding myself doing overtime and alone in the building, I got on my knees and told the Lord that I was without strength and didn't know what to do. When I got home, after being in the flat only five minutes, the phone rang, and it was John Darroch suggesting we come up to Wycombe to live. After hanging up I burst into tears. I resigned not long after.

By the providence of God we moved, found jobs and somewhere to live, and began to attend the meetings of the saints. It was then that I began to feel enmity against all things godly and although God's mercy toward me was so manifest, yet I was locked in desperation and unbelief. Doubts would attack me, one particularly strong one that was always with me was that the Lord had only called my brother and that I had somehow become emotionally caught up in it and was only deluding myself. When exhorted to begin to pray in the meetings, I was shocked, thinking, How can I pray, I'm not saved? I did pray a few times but stopped because I felt a hypocrite, saying to myself, When I'm saved then I'll pray, glad of a plausible excuse not to do so. Thus I did nothing; I felt that I waited upon the Lord, waited for salvation to begin. Any suggestions to believe I greeted with confusion, saying to myself, What do they think I am, an Arminian?

This went on a long time, unconsciously building barriers against the salvation of God, secretly not wanting to be saved. Resisting the Holy Ghost, blocking his sweet sensations by saying, These can't be from God, I'm not saved. Even when told the Spirit shall not always strive with man, I wouldn't receive it.

But the Lord in his great mercy caused me to hear Mr. Metcalfe preach on Rom. 10:13, 'Whosoever shall call upon the name of the Lord shall be saved.' How that word spoke directly to my state! How I saw I was excluding myself! How I saw that I was waiting for a special vision of Christ as my Saviour before I'd believe! How I saw that I was saying, 'Who shall ascend into heaven?' and 'Who shall descend into the deep?' The barriers crumbled away and disappeared: I knew I'd been saved; all the experiences that before only led me into self-pity, now began to shout and proclaim the mercy of God toward me, the sensations of the Holy Ghost now came into my soul, I understood for the first time what Faith was. I had been brought to Faith.

Within days strong doubts began to shake me, so much so that I was almost back into the old way of unbelief, starting to think that it was all presumption and that I must wait upon the Lord, and not believe anything. I was in such confusion I prayed to my God and Father that he would show me the right path to take. Immediately my prayer was answered, and I thank and praise his holy name for his mercy and grace toward me.

Now my prayer to the Father is that I may grow in grace and in the knowledge of our Lord and Saviour Jesus Christ. Believing that only because Christ had taken my sins upon himself and borne my punishment in his own body, could the God of all righteousness call me out of darkness into the light of the truth through the preaching of the gospel.

Stephen Luford

The Conversion of
Coralie Barker

High Wycombe,
Bucks.

The earlier years of my life were not very happy ones. At five years old I was separated from my mother and taken to St. Vincent, an Island in the West Indies. In St. Vincent I lived with my aunt, who attended the Gospel Hall.

During the ten years that I lived in St. Vincent I learned many bible stories and had to memorise verses of scripture which at that time didn't really mean anything to me. Almost every Sunday night the coming of the Lord was preached and after that there would be the persuasion of the preacher to accept Christ. Nearly every Sunday night when I got home I would cry to the Lord to save my soul.

Being under the impression that a Christian was perfect and seeing no change in me each time, I gave up on being saved. I was never taught anything concerning the law, predestination or election. I even went up to the front to accept Jesus, as they called it, but nothing happened.

After ten years I returned to England, but before leaving St. Vincent my dad promised my aunt that we would continue going to a Gospel Hall in this country. I attended the Gospel Hall in this country for a few months and it wasn't long before

I was being persuaded into becoming a Christian. The Gospel Hall to me was a dead and boring place. After a short time I left.

For a few months I didn't go anywhere. Then for no reason I started to attend a Roman Catholic place. I never got anything out of it, but I thought as long as I went somewhere it was alright. While still in the Catholic place I got involved with my next door neighbours, who attended the Baptist place. I then left the Catholic place and went to the Baptist place. Because the Baptist place allowed me to hold on to the world and have fun, I was soon swept into it. I made my decision concerning Christ, as they put it. I had the world and lots of friends and fun and that suited me fine.

But I soon began to not want all the good things they offered. I began to feel the need to take the Lord more seriously. I began to feel the convictions of God and my soul was in agony and felt as if it was being crushed. I soon began to doubt that I was saved and that God existed. I mentioned this to one of the young people there, who looked at me with surprise. I soon began to try and live a good life but I couldn't, the weight of the law weighed heavy on my soul, but each day I lived as its slave, knowing no better. I got very depressed because all the other Baptists always seemed happy and content. In this state I was baptised, after nine months.

Earlier this year (1986) I was shown Romans 7 by my mother and for the first time I knew something of what living under the law was, I was able to understand some of what Paul said because it was my experience. Through listening to tapes and reading a few books I was confronted with the gospel and instead of accepting it I avoided it because it was different and because it showed me my true condition. I tried to get it out of my mind but it wouldn't leave me alone. I tried desperately to hold on to my pretence salvation and my works but they couldn't stand. I was stripped of everything I thought I had.

After three months of struggling to hold on to what I thought I had, I finally let it all go. However, I didn't leave the Baptist place for fear of man. While going there I read the two magazines I had and also some of the books. During this time I was convicted because I knew the truth but for fear of man I went along with them. I had no peace in me: all I could see was condemnation for my disobedience. I soon began to hate their awful barn dances and so called Christian concerts and then I began to detest their company. Their false niceness made me feel quite ill. During that time the Lord opened my eyes to see their lies and pretence, but because of my disobedience I was soon blinded again. Every day I went to the Baptist place I lived in fear of being struck dead because I was being disobedient.

But I praise God for his mercy and patience towards me and that even after my disobedience he opened my eyes to his truth. While reading the address by J.C. Philpot in the Autumn magazine, I realised that the Baptist and all the other worldly churches did not separate the precious from the vile. Instead they would join with any person who said they were a Christian, and that they never exposed any false religion, nor can they, because they are not preachers chosen by God, but preachers taught and chosen by man, who preach what pleases man. I knew that they were enemies of Christ and that I could never go to that place again.

Thank God that although men have disapproved, I haven't gone back to their lies. Praise God for the awakening of my soul to turn from easy-believism to the true God and also that I wasn't turned to a reprobate mind. I now know that my prayers all those years ago were not in vain. Now, through his called preachers, I can hear his words of life for the salvation of my soul. Now I don't just think I believe, I know I believe although the devil tries to keep me in unbelief. I believe that when Jesus died, in him my sins died, and when he was raised from the dead, I rose in him.

Coralie Barker

The Conversion of
Robert Luford

High Wycombe,
Bucks.

4th August, 1989

Dear Mr. Metcalfe,

Truly I thank and bless God our Father and the Lord Jesus Christ that ever I'm in a position to write unto thee of the dealings of God in my soul. Though my testimony thus far might sound as Naomi's, 'the LORD hath testified against me, and the Almighty hath afflicted me'. Yet what mercy that God should deign to look upon me.

As a child I stamped out of my conscience the light of God and often told myself there is no God. As a fool I lived saying, Who shall see it? For all that, I remember at quite a young age, twelve or thirteen years, having a strong fear and forboding of death, and a sense of futility. These things however were of no avail in checking my sinful ways and for the most part I lived in complete ignorance. Dead to God and to 'life'. Truly our lives are death before we're awakened.

My parents emigrated in 1963 taking my two brothers and myself to Melbourne where we lived for a year at a hostel and then moved up to Sydney, where we eventually bought a house. Due to their desires of returning to England and a restlessness within myself, drifting from job to job, aimless, careless, seeking pleasure, my brother and I came to London. My parents returned while we were here, but we didn't like England and were very homesick, although actually for a place that was no longer home. However we returned. Due to this 'homelessness' I crossed the world five times, each time the sense of nightmare becoming stronger, misery, despair filled my life. No sooner would I land and try to settle, England or Australia, but there would arise a sense of uneasiness, an aching emptiness and deep distress.

During our first attempt to live in Sydney, Stephen began to look, only cursorily I think, at Christianity. We'd both been interested in 'eastern mysticism' as it's called. My generation, due to the evil introduction of what are called 'consciousness expanding' drugs, had been snared by this 'religion'. As much by the language and the clothes as anything. It was the constant comparisons of the teachings of these men with the teachings of Christ that drew Stephen towards the bible. Perhaps unconsciously they had set up the truth as a yardstick for their own philosophy.

About this time we heard a young man singing and preaching in the High Street of the suburb where we lived. We stopped to listen. Afterwards he came over to us and, amongst other things, he told me that except a man believes in Jesus Christ he'll surely be burned for ever in hell. This was not something he had made up, it was in the bible. Deep within I believed this was true, I bought a bible and tried to make a profession. Unbelief was so strong in me that it almost prevailed completely. The fool hath said in his heart, There is no God. I tried, and for a while shut out this truth of the wrath to come. It haunted me and on top of this sense of hopelessness, made my life extremely bitter.

We returned to England, I think it was 1980. My parents were living in Dorset, just outside Bournemouth. Being near a very old village, I was attracted to the Anglican steeplehouse, still holding on to some kind of profession of the name of Jesus. I had not repented or changed my life in any way and, for the most part, was in complete bondage and unbelief. It was during an address at this place that I first, in quite an unusual way, came to know your name. If asked to remember anything spoken in that place, I'd have to say one thing only: 'There is no scientific evidence to prove the flood.' I knew I was afflicted by unbelief but I was staggered. What do they believe then?

I wanted to know about the flood and if the reaction of Christendom to this truth was the same as that of this clergyman. The very first book I found in the religious bookshop in Bournemouth was called 'Noah and the Flood'. Praise the Lord! However at the time I found within myself a mixed reaction. For the one thing I received from this book was an even more certain conviction of the wrath to come. I stopped going to 'church' and sank in despair.

Gradually I bought more of your books, and a great sense of fear lay upon me. I was convinced that because of my unbelief I couldn't be reached. There is no God: this was pressed so hard into me that once again I gave up and shut everything out. This time falling deeper into depravity than ever before. I returned to Australia, alone, broken and shattered, feeling I'd lived far too long already. For about two years I tried to live under the law, and then, if my convictions waned, lawless.

As the time approached for my return to England, I began to cry out to God for mercy from sheer desperation and despair. I cancelled. I couldn't go through with it, but I had no work to return to. Forced by circumstances, I had to leave Australia once again. Thanks be unto God, I never returned. I found work and a bedsitting room and once again I tried to shut out the existence of God and of judgment to come. My convictions returned and coincided with an explosion of a nuclear reactor in Russia. I was terrified, trembling, unable to sleep, crying out with all my might for mercy and forgiveness. The event passed, my convictions wore off; back again in the world. I had thrown away all my worldly possessions during this time.

Intermittently my convictions would return and alarm me, yet no sooner would they fade and I would return, like the sow that was washed, to my vomit. Each time convinced that there could be no mercy for such a reprobate. About six months before I really repented, left the world, and began in earnest to seek the Lord, I was walking along the cliffs and a most fearful frame came upon me. I was alive upon the earth amidst infinite space alone, all people alone on the earth, blind, lost without God. It stayed with me for some time. I couldn't comprehend or understand that these strange frames and sensations were the consequences of the influences of the Holy Spirit.

In January 1988, sitting in a friend's house in London, I began to reason thus, The only way I'm going to get free of these things is to seek the Lord. Strange it seems now. I was reading a novel and the name of the Lord was mentioned and within me it was as if a voice said 'Seek the Lord'. I came back to my flat and threw out everything that was worldly and of the world, television, radio, books, everything. I began to read your books again and bought 'Christ Crucified' and 'Justification by Faith'. Once again the wrath came with power and I began to cry out and confess my sins. About March I sent for a magazine and whilst reading 'A Dying Witness' wept as I read, seeing so much of my state in hers. A list of the tapes was with the magazine. It had been on my mind about this time, as I beheld the beauty of the earth and the sea and all that God had created, to know more, so, seeing a tape entitled 'God revealed in Creation', I sent for it.

Truly, Mr. Metcalfe, all that had happened to me so far was just the gathering of dark clouds on the horizon and soon the storm would come. As I listened, the 'wrath of God was

revealed from heaven against all ungodliness and unrighteousness of men who hold the truth in unrighteousness', but
not just outwardly, it was revealed inwardly to me. I fell to
the floor as a nightmare of panic and fear filled me, roaring
and crying. All night crying out, walking the streets, trembling, holding my stomach. God was angry, I felt it. His hand
pressed me sore. The following day the sensations stronger:
nothing but terrible wrath.

I awoke on Monday about five a.m. trembling and praying,
weeping for hours. I couldn't go to work, I rang my boss and
resigned and told him I couldn't return to work. I wandered
the cliffs, praying and crying out for mercy. At times I'd try
to go out but would immediately return, my stomach on fire,
seemingly unable to walk and I'd lie on my bed and cry to the
Lord. On Wednesday I felt I'd entered a nightmare from which
I'd never wake, I know now I'd been awakened to reality. I
rang the Trust, a woman answered. I told her my experience,
she suggested I write. But I wanted to talk with someone. I
found John Darroch's number on a letter he'd written in
answer to a query I'd made about the 'Book of Ruth', I'd
wanted to purchase it after reading 'A Famine in the Land'.
This was the famine I felt in myself. John suggested I come to
Penn, I agreed.

As I entered John's house the presence of God came into my
soul, I knew that these were God's people. The Lord in his
mercy had led me to where his people were being gathered. On
one level I could see this, yet the overriding feeling was wrath
and judgment. I attended the meeting, a prayer meeting on the
Saturday evening. Here I saw a serious, sober, God-fearing
people. A company I could never have been with, without
the same fear and sense of the majesty of the Lord, he that
hath made all things. I returned to Bournemouth, quieter but
was soon groaning and crying after listening to the tapes that
arrived that week: Ephesians 2:8 I remember well.

97

After much prayer about the course to take and an incident that left me penniless, still jobless, and full of gloom, an answer to our prayers came. John phoned Stephen and suggested we move up to Wycombe. We agreed. Within a month or so we were renting this house and trying to buy a property. Attending the meetings, I was full of fear and truly I've never stopped calling out day and night for mercy and salvation. Though at times I've been brought to question whether such things are possible for me. Oh, my soul, Trust thou in the Lord.

Many things I've been taught, and I know that in me the mountains and hills must be brought low and the valleys exalted. The way seems hidden to me but 'I will bring the blind by a way that they knew not; I will lead them in paths that they have not known: I will make darkness light before them, and crooked things straight. These things will I do unto them, and not forsake them.' This is my comfort in all my afflictions: 'and not forsake them'. Though I'm so unfaithful, unbelieving, yet I hope in God's mercy and that I'll yet praise him from a heart that loves because he has loved me. All I cry for is to say from my heart 'Christ loved me and gave himself for me.'

As I prolonged concluding and sending this letter, I give thanks every day that there is more to be said. Putting my pen down I bowed before my God and Father thanking him for his mercy towards me. Still the gospel came to me after all that, and the Lord works within me, I feel it. I believe that Jesus Christ came in the flesh. He who is from everlasting God the Son who came of the seed of David according to the flesh. And declared to be the Son of God with power, according to the Spirit of holiness, by the resurrection from the dead. 'From the dead'; Christ died! Yea is risen again. Now at the right hand of God and the Father. What a glorious gospel this is, that declares such things. Oh, that I might see in the death of Christ my death, an answer to all that stands between God and myself, to see that all I am is judged and condemned and destroyed in the death of Jesus Christ on the cross. Amen.

Yours sincerely,
Robert Luford

High Wycombe,
Bucks.
10th August, 1989

Dear Mr. Metcalfe,

When I gave my previous letter to John to pass on to you last first day, it was with much fear and trembling, feeling myself again shut up in helpless unbelief.

On Monday I was almost in despair, my unbelief crushing my spirit, I broke down and poured out my complaint before the Lord in the morning at work, great crying and groaning.

At the brethren's meeting for prayer that Monday evening, I felt the same, still groaning to be delivered from this bondage. I was! For the first time ever, I could say and believe that Christ loved me and gave himself for me. Thanks be unto God. Though I falter, nevertheless, 'If thou shalt confess with thy mouth the Lord Jesus, and shalt believe in thine heart that God hath raised him from the dead, thou shalt be saved.'

To God only wise, be glory, through Jesus Christ for ever. Amen.

Yours sincerely,
Robert Luford

In Labours More Abundant

AFTER the early period of building up the work at Tylers Green by preaching and teaching the gospel, Mr. Metcalfe was called to the momentous work that took over six years of his life in isolation and seclusion writing in metre The Psalms of the Old Testament (published January 1985), the Songs from the Gospels (published March 1985) and the Hymns of the New Testament (published September 1985). As a result of this unique and inspired work scripture itself is sung, not error and sentiment contrary to the word of Christ.

Mr. Metcalfe's back suffered much from the long hours spent in the strained and intense posture brought on by such concentration in writing, so much so that had he not received prompt and expert treatment in the Far East he would have become completely immobile. Out of such pain and so prolonged a time of travail came this heavenly service, in the will of God enabling the true worshippers at last to obey Christ and the apostles in the singing of psalms, hymns, and spiritual songs.

In 1984, before Mr. Metcalfe had completed the Psalms, Hymns and Songs, he was called to preach for several weeks in South-East Asia. The Lord blessed the word preached as many among his hearers have testified. Mr. Metcalfe returned to England in January 1985, physically exhausted, having given himself in labour for the salvation of souls in that alien, tropical climate, amidst the opposition and persecutions which always accompany the faithful preaching of the word. On more than one occasion, when he was back in England, he fainted from sheer exhaustion.

However, many in Asia pressed him to return to minister among them and the Lord's mind was sought both privately and in the congregations, beseeching him that his will should be made plain. At the same time Mr. Metcalfe was working day and night to finish the Hymns of the New Testament, as well as to fulfil those other cares which came upon him daily in connection with the assemblies.

Mr. Metcalfe left England to begin preaching and teaching the gospel in Singapore and Malaysia on July 17th 1985. The servant of God laboured long and hard in much physical weakness under adverse conditions in the humid and debilitating climate of South-East Asia. Nevertheless this brought forth much fruit.

The following few selected testimonies bear record of this, and to Mr. Metcalfe's subsequent labours in the Far East.

The Testimony of
Yeo Cheung Gheem

Singapore
26th July, 1989

Dear Mr. Metcalfe,

Thank you so much for the word of God preached in Penang. We are hearing the tapes again and they seem even more clear than when first heard. In fact, each time when I hear the tapes again, they are so much more powerful and so refreshing.

My heart truly rejoices in the marvellous works of God. Though unworthy as I am, I am very grateful to be brought into the way of the ancient landmarks by which our fathers were led and according to which they first trod—to be shown those ancient pathways and boundary stones, and to be led into them by his blessed Holy Spirit, this is truly too marvellous in my sight.

As I pondered over the works of God and considered all that he had done in my life, I thought it meet that I should write to you of what God had done for me.

I was brought up in a rather staunch Taoist family, in a kampong; whilst there I was educated in a convent. I continued my education in another convent when I shifted out into the new town. It was not until I was in secondary one (about 13 years old) that I was told about Jesus by some of my friends. A small group of my friends (about three or four young girls) started a sort of bible study group called a 'cell group'. Those that attended 'church' would sometimes share with us what they had learnt and heard, but most of the time, we spent the time sharing or singing 'hymns'. I was one of those that would attend their meetings after school secretly, not daring to let my parents know.

When I was in secondary two (about 14 years old) something happened within my family that really shook me up. I can't remember how it happened or why it happened but my mother tried to commit suicide. I remembered coming home from school to see my house in a commotion and my mother crying. I was shocked when I learnt what had happened. The children were blamed for the incident on account of being naughty, but I doubt it was this. We were made to kneel before her to ask for forgiveness. Stunned, I just did it. I kept asking myself, Why did my mother want to do such a thing? What would happen if she should die? Where would she go? It just frightened me to think of death.

I remembered going to school the next day, confused, and I cried and confided in one of my friends, an Anglican girl, and she told me to accept Jesus as my Saviour, and he will help me. Out of desperateness, I did it and prayed the 'sinner's prayer' as they called it. But after doing that, I felt no change at all, and my problem was still there. I was really miserable.

I think I went on like this for some time (I can't remember how long) until one day I couldn't take it any more. And being left alone that night in the house, I went and bowed down before the Taoist altar with their gods and prayed that if they be the true gods, to tell me. Then I went to the bedroom (which I shared with my parents, sister and brother) and to my bed, and knelt and prayed to Jesus, that if he were the true God, to tell me and show me the truth. Then I cried till I slept.

Deep within me I knew there was a true God, but I didn't know which one. I didn't attend any 'church' but I did visit the idols' temples sometimes with my parents.

During my secondary school days, I would also attend this 'cell group' regularly. Whenever there was opportunity I would find time outside my home to read the bible. I usually sought solace in the catholic chapel, next to my school, during recess times. My first bible was a K.J.V. (Authorized Version) given to me by a Seventh Day Adventist girl. I had difficulty trying to read it because I wasn't used to the older English as I supposed then. I was told to try the Living Bible but instinctively I didn't like it. I was also told to use other versions but because of lack of finance, I had to use my K.J.V. first.

Despite the difficulty, I just loved reading the Book of Psalms. Maybe it was because I could see, in some small measure, eye to eye with the experience of the psalmist.

As the years went by, I felt more and more convinced that this Jesus, whom I'd heard and read of, was the true God. I remembered reading in one of the psalms about the idols which the heathen worship—having mouths but they spoke not, eyes but saw not, ears but they heard not, noses but smelled not. And I remembered feeling within myself how true these things were and how ridiculous that men should bow down to a god made by their own hands! How can it be a god then?

It was not till I was in secondary four (about 16 years old) that I felt I can't go on denying what I've believed. I felt that since I've embraced Christianity, I ought to confess it and not be a hypocrite. In fact, my conscience very often troubled me when I bowed down before the idols, holding the joss-sticks. I wanted to stop doing it but I found no courage to do so. I really felt so hypocritical.

One day, early in the morning, I was awakened by my mother, to wash myself and go to pray to my 'god' mother (the idol goddess of mercy) as it was 'her' birthday. I tried to avoid it by pretending to sleep but my mother dragged me out of bed.

But I just couldn't do it. I felt a strong prompting within me to make a stand. I felt all strength not to compromise even though my mother had gone from the room. I just couldn't bring myself to hold the joss-sticks and to bow before the idol goddess. I went and told my mother, I don't want to pray to her gods and I don't want to hold the joss-sticks any more.

The fury that lit up in her face was enough to scare the daylight out of me but I marvel at the courage granted unto me to stand at that time. I was literally dragged to the altar and the joss-sticks were thrust before my face as I was told to bow and pray. I refused to do so and wrung free from my mother.

When my mother saw my stubbornness, she called my father and took the cane and said, she will beat me to death. My mother really caned me till she's tired. Then my father shouted and scolded me for daring to change my religion without his approval. In between sobs, I told my father that I'm old enough to decide on my own beliefs. But that answer really blew his top.

Then I was locked up at home and forbidden to go to school any more. My mother told me that they will not allow me to sit for the 'O' levels and no more school for me. I was crying non-stop, but when I heard that, my heart really sank. To me, going to school was like a door of freedom. Within my heart, I told the Lord, I can't take it. To stay at home was like a torture as I knew that every movement that I made would be watched. The thought of not being able to read God's word and to have some time of quietness was utterly heart-breaking.

It happened on a Friday and the next two days were the week-end, but I was locked in and forbidden to go out at all. I was really miserable.

But thanks be unto God for his compassion and love, for that following Monday, my parents relented (to my great surprise) and allowed me to go to school. (I think my grandma talked to them.) I was so glad to be freed.

But when I reached school, I couldn't help but burst out into tears when I thought how short this liberty might be—not knowing what the next day might bring forth. I told one of my friends what had happened and said that I might not be able to see her or them again.

But thanks be unto God, who didn't try me beyond that which I'm able to bear, but did make a way of escape for me. I was allowed to go back to school and to complete my education. I was really very grateful unto God for his kindness.

What really filled my heart with joy, was the fact that after that incident, my parents didn't try to make me to hold the joss-sticks any more nor force me to burn the incense nor demand that I should bow to their idols. I was really glad for the deliverance—because, knowing them, I would have thought that they would force me again the next time, but they didn't. It was just marvellous how the Lord worked.

After the 'O' levels, I went to a catholic junior college. In college, our 'cell group' still continued and as it had grown larger, we felt we ought to get someone to conduct proper bible study. One of my friends, who was the niece of Peter Ng, the founder of the 'Jesus Saves' Mission, recommended a 'JSM' missioner to us.

But despite all these things (the 'cell group' and bible studies) my heart yearned to go to a true 'church'. I felt that it was time that I should attend a 'church'. This yearning and desire was so strong that I felt I must do it despite what it might cost me.

It was not until I was in Pre. U. II (about 18 years old) that I took courage to do so. I remembered that Sunday morning when I woke up. The desire and fear that was upon my heart, I know not how to express. Brushing aside my fears, I told myself that it was now or never. I quickly got up, washed, had my breakfast, and changed. I told my mother that I was going to 'church'. My mother told me to go and tell my father and sternly told me not to go, or else. I was quite frightened and I went back to the room and hesitated. But my sister, who heard it, whispered to me to go ahead. When I heard that, I felt I must go, all the more. I went to the door, but before opening it, I politely told my father and mother that I was going to 'church'. I could feel the immense tension that had built up at that time, waiting to burst forth. I waited a while before I closed the door quietly. While I was about to go down the stairs, my father suddenly opened the door and shouted at me never to come back home again and slammed the door so hard that I could feel as if the whole block shook.

I was shocked. As I walked down the stairs, I couldn't control the tears that kept rolling down from my eyes. I just couldn't believe that my father would drive me out of the house.

Actually, when I went out of the house, I really had no idea which 'church' I should go to. I didn't tell my friends about it nor did I make prior arrangements with them. I don't know why. But I did commit it to God to lead me to the true 'church'. In the end, since I've only the 'Jesus Saves' Mission address, I decided to go to 'JSM'.

The first impression that I had of 'JSM' was of coldness and strangeness. After the 'service', everybody just talked and later dispersed to their own groups. I felt so left out. My heart was so heavy and so disappointed. I asked the Lord whether I've come to the right 'church'. My heart was near breaking and I wished I could talk to someone to ask for counsel but there was none. Though my bible study teacher was there, I just couldn't bring myself to approach him.

At that moment, I really felt as if all that effort and stand that I'd made, seemed to be wasted. I felt rejected both by God and men. I kept asking God, Why? Why lead me into this place, to feel rejected by them? I felt so confused; not knowing what to do next. It seemed like an irony.

After much thought, I decided to go back home and see how the situation was. If my family refused to open the door or if my father drove me out again, I told the Lord that I would take it as his will and would not return again. But if they opened up and didn't drive me away, then, I'd stay and face the consequences.

When I reached home, I was rather frightened to knock at the door, but, summoning up my courage, I knocked quietly for quite some time. I was about to go off, when my younger brother opened the door for me. As I entered the house, I could feel the tension, coldness and enmity within, so much so that I wished I had not returned. My parents, especially my father, refused to look at me or talk to me. Later on, my mother brought me to the room and I was scolded and interrogated by both my mother and grandmother. I kept quiet most of the time, not daring to cry in front of them, but my heart was near bursting. I learnt from them that my father had intended to beat me up if I should step into the house again but was persuaded not to do so by them.

After that I was interrogated by my father. The fury that was written on his face was really scary. I just sat there trembling. As he talked, I could sense that he was trying to control his anger. I couldn't remember what he told me but I could remember this that he said to me—that if I should ever regret and turn away from my belief, he'll never forgive me nor acknowledge me as his daughter even if I should beg him. At first I couldn't understand what he was trying to tell me as he is a person who always likes to beat around the bush when talking. His statement seemed so contradictory. Later, I realised that he was actually denying me as his daughter. That was the last statement he made. I was really hurt. I told my father that I will not deny my belief. And he just walked away.

But I remembered this verse in Ps. 27:10 which says that when my father and my mother forsake me, then the LORD will take me up. How true it is and I could feel and see for myself how often the LORD would take me up and cause me not to be cast down, especially when my parents treated me with such contempt and at times literally hatred.

I remembered how, after that incident, my father never talked to me, but treated me as if I didn't exist at all. Despite all these things, I still treated my parents with respect as I ought to. I still made drinks for my father each evening (which I usually do) but each time I did it, my father would pour it away, even in front of me. I was really hurt that he should hate me so. Ever since then, I decided not to make drinks for him, not because I wanted to retaliate but because I found it useless. I felt it was better that I should keep a low profile.

But trouble did not end there. In fact, this was the beginning of many new trials. Since I'd made that stand, I decided to persevere in going to 'church' each Sunday, though at times, I really dreaded going to 'JSM'. I was quite put off by the coldness of the people and the superficiality. I decided to try other 'churches'. But I didn't like them as they seem too frivolous and light. Comparing them to 'JSM', I felt that 'JSM' was the more sober and disciplined. But I was miserable there.

One day, while I was walking to college alone, I was so miserable that I cried to God within my heart, for help. I don't want to stop going to 'church', since I've made that stand, for I knew that my parents would then laugh at my fall and I felt God's name is at stake. But I also didn't feel like going to 'JSM', seeing the people there were so strange.

As I was complaining to God, these questions suddenly came to me: What are you actually seeking for? Is it for the fellowship of men? To be seen of and sympathised by men? Or is it to seek the face of God and him only? These questions really shook me up from my self pity. And, as to what my actual cause of wanting to go to 'church', I was really put to shame to see the deceitfulness of my heart.

Then I told myself to stop complaining and grumbling. If my sole aim and purpose was to seek God and to worship him in the 'church' then why did I worry about how the people treated me? Let them be, but just go and seek God. The peace that filled my heart, when the thoughts of my heart were made known, was really marvellous. I asked the Lord for forgiveness and decided to set my heart to seek his face only.

My parents never left me alone. After attending 'JSM' for a few months, my parents decided to visit 'JSM' to see what it was. I tried to disuade them, knowing that they will make a commotion there. I told them that it has got nothing to do with them as it is my faith and belief. But whatever I said fell on deaf ears. It seemed that they almost quarrelled with a certain missioner, when he came and talked to them.

But this visit was not the last but the beginning of many such visits to 'JSM' (even up to when it had closed down). Throughout the six years that I was in 'JSM', my parents would never leave me alone. I was even trailed by them to the meetings. At home, there was no peace either, as I was often scolded and threatened by them. They even came to the extent of thinking I was possessed with an evil spirit. They would go to the mediums to ask for charm papers. These are burnt and their ashes put into the drinks or food. I was given it without my knowledge. I only found out one day, while I was drinking the water, when I saw some residue of ashes in the cup. I was quite angry with my parents and I approached my mother and told her not to do that again. But I committed these things unto the Lord, knowing that my God is greater than theirs, and that my trust is in him alone. I knew that no 'charm' can harm those that are his.

Throughout all these times, I know that it was the Lord that had kept and preserved me. As I consider all these things, I felt no regret for all that the Lord had brought me through. In fact, I'm very very grateful for all my trials and I wouldn't want to exchange any of them for anything in this world.

It was not until 1984 that I actually thought upon these things that had come upon my way. It was not something that I'd asked for but it just happened. I felt as if God were preparing me for something but I don't know what it was. Since 'JSM' stresses so much on 'calling', I actually thought, maybe, the Lord is preparing me for so-called 'full-time service'. I didn't tell anyone about that until the latter part of 1984. But when it fell on the missioner's ears, he never let me go, but really hounded me about 'my calling'. I told him I'm not sure and I'm not ready. But he said that I'm trying to run away from God's calling. I was really confused and I felt trapped.

It came to pass at that time that there was a conference on Penang Hill. This was in December, 1984, where you were asked to preach. I could only attend the latter part of the conference. Before I went up to Penang, I asked the Lord to show me clearly what his will was, so great was my confusion.

I remembered the first message that I heard from you was on 'Justification by Faith' on Rom. 3:28. Though I couldn't really understand it, I just loved that spirit that is in you. The joy that lights up your face as you preached it was so real that I told the Lord that I would like to have that selfsame spirit and that joy that is in you. It was so different from other preaching that I've heard.

Because of your coming to Penang and to Singapore, 'my calling' was temporarily taken off the missioner's mind, for which I was most glad. After that, because of the other incidents that followed, this so-called full-time service was forgotten. I felt this was a providence of God and I'm very grateful for being delivered out of that system of bondage and oppression.

It is really amazing how the Lord leads each one of his people and gathers us as one company unto himself. It is like what was preached on Psalm 84 wherein the psalmist set out alone but later found a company with him of which 'every one of them in Zion appeareth before God'.

When I heard the message on Jn. 1:23 on the works of John the Baptist, I couldn't help but feel that these are the preparatory works of God in my heart and in my own experience. Of my own self, I know I wouldn't have chosen this pathway. Neither did I ever think or dream of being brought into this blessed privilege, to be under this true gospel ministry. It is truly nothing but grace and grace alone! How amazing and marvellous is his love! It is just too wonderful for me, seeing what manner of person I am, that God should love me so, and give his only begotten Son, to die on the cross for me.

Truly, what is man that God should take knowledge of him? He has not only wrought forth salvation for me, but even condescended to lead me (who am really nothing, but a stinking body filled with putrifying corruption and filthiness) through this pathway with such love and longsuffering unto such a wealthy place in Christ Jesus. Oh, how really amazing and beyond comprehension!

I am very grateful and thankful unto God for all that he has done in my life. Truly, none teacheth like him! But, I do not wish to dwell nor rest in past experiences and deliverances, for there's still much, much more to learn of Christ. Desiring to be made truly empty of all that pertaineth to the flesh (in all its consciousness and sensitivity) that Christ alone be my all in all. O, that my whole being be taken up for his glory alone!

Mr. Metcalfe, please pray for me. (I know you do but I can't help asking for it.)

Thank you so much for this ministry and for bringing this gospel truth into out midst, despite and in spite of the circumstances of your terrible trials and betrayals at that very time. Thank you for being so long-suffering with us throughout these years and for your constant love.

We are all praying for you and for the going forth of the gospel, desiring to see the truth being brought unto many, many souls and many, many countries.

The Lord be with thee and bless thee.

In His everlasting love,
Cheung Gheem

To: Yeo Cheung Gheem
From: John Metcalfe

High Wycombe,
Bucks.

2nd August, 1989

My dearly beloved daughter in the faith,

Grace be unto thee, mercy and peace, from God our Father and the Lord Jesus Christ.

Your letter and testimony which came today, melted my heart, made my eyes a fountain of tears, filled my mouth with praise and thanksgiving, and ministered to me abundantly from the grace of God and our Father through Jesus Christ our Lord.

I believe and am sure that the Lord guided you to send your testimony at this time that you might be a consolation and comfort to me in the Spirit, which you have been in truth. To write spiritually—as I am now doing—and with that carefulness in the word of God which comes not only from meticulous discipline in scripture—though that must be there—but from a feeling sensitiveness to the anointing, unction, and leading of the Holy One within: Oh, this is so exhausting. It is like being picked up and wrung out of all moisture: not so much whilst one is writing, but immediately one stops. Then the sense of being drained, and used up, sweeps over one, as if more than one possessed had been given out in the work.

So it was this morning when your letter came, and truly I can say that it was as clear fresh water in a dry and thirsty land.

Forgive me, my dear Cheung Gheem, for the shortness of my reply. I am in the midst of travail over the present book, literally wrung out and exhausted, and yet I must keep on, not sparing myself in this work: hence, time and energy are short.

My abiding love and care for you in Christ, and the assurance that you are graven on my heart in thanksgiving, prayer and intercession.

Remember me also when thou goest to the throne of grace.

Ever your devoted minister,

John Metcalfe

The Conversion of Cindy Lee Lye Sim

Singapore

10th June, 1990

I was a fool that said in my heart 'There is no God', for I had lived out the early years of my life in ungodliness. My childhood days were spent in much ease and pleasure. I had no religion. The times which I had anything to do with something near religion was when my grandmother desired me to help her in preparing the joss papers. At a certain time of the year, she remembers the death of her ancestors. Much food would be prepared and laid on a table with lighted candles on the forefront of the table. She would pull me along with her to kneel and bow before the table of food and candles with joss sticks in my hand. The joss papers were burnt later. Each time when I was made to do it, an uncomfortable feeling was in me. I suppose it was more of pride that I felt ridiculous, being found in such a posture.

I remember an incident at school. The senior teacher raised a question at a school assembly. She asked for a show of hands of those who believed the existence of God. A number of hands were raised but I laughed and scorned at them and said to myself—there is no God. I was twelve years old then.

That which occupied me at the time was satisfying my greedy appetite for food, having fun and school. Not that I was studious. I had favours from teachers because of my brother. In that way, I was to maintain a reputation as a good student for the honour of my parents. I was a self-righteous hypocrite in school. My head was filled with pride—thinking myself to be something. The mischiefs I did in secret were hid from teachers. I was a liar and a talebearer. I was disobedient to my parents with rebellion in the heart when punished. I hated work and I was delighted at every opportunity to escape any house chores.

The fear of hell took hold of me when I was thirteen. My brother met a young man at the Stadium in a sports meet, who told him of sin, death, hell and of Jesus Christ the Saviour. When my brother came home, he related all that he heard to us. I was convinced of hell. My brother was very sober and serious when he spoke those words, which was unlike him. I went away and in secret prayed the 'sinner's prayer'

115

which was to confess one's sins, to ask for forgiveness for one's sins, to open one's heart and to accept Jesus into the heart as Saviour. But there was no peace in my heart. Whenever I felt that fear, I repeated the 'sinner's prayer'. I tried to cast away my fears by occupying myself with something to do but was not successful.

After some time, I could not contain it any more. I spoke to my brother and told him my trouble. He enquired whether I had prayed the 'sinner's prayer'. I replied I had done so and many times over. He suggested attending the meetings—'worship service' and Sunday school at 'JSM', where he had already been. He also instructed me to read the Bible daily. So I kept up Bible reading, as conscientiously as I could, for I felt if I failed to, I would have sinned. But I could not understand what I read and soon it became a weariness.

It was much later that I attended the service and Sunday school, being hindered by my mother—not that she was against the Christian religion but more so for my safety. Before that, I had almost involved myself in becoming a member of the 'Youth For Christ' group, after having met a few members in one of their meetings. This went on without my mother's knowledge during school hours. Two of my classmates were with that group and persuaded me to join them and which I did. My brother discovered the matter and warned me to leave, to which I submitted.

It was after much persuasion and assurance from my brother, that my mother allowed me to go to the meetings at the Mission. I did not attend the 'worship service' in the morning regularly. I had difficulty understanding the message the 'reverend' or a brother gave. Besides I felt quite lost when I was there. I was separated from my brother. He had to sit on a different row of benches from me as the men and women had to be seated on different rows. Sunday school was better to me for at least I could receive some knowledge and understanding of the Bible. I was still troubled about my salvation.

Someone from the Mission showed and explained to me from I John chapter 5, verse 13, that it is a matter of believing and knowing and not according to feelings, when I told her my feelings and questions on the salvation of my soul. Hence, this became my answer each time my doubts arose.

Later, to my disappointment, I learnt that there were 'dos' and 'don'ts' which were expected of us to keep. Two of which I found great difficulty giving them up. That was the television and cinema. In the afternoon, after Sunday school, I was back home, in front of the television. There were times my brother invited people from the Mission to the house. Whenever I knew they were coming, or heard their voices from outside the house, how I hurried to shut the television and hid myself in the room. I felt rotten and guilty of such hypocrisy. I was a television addict and to me it was impossible to leave it off.

I was baptized by a 'reverend' the next year. Soon afterwards, I grew weary. Much of my time and energy were spent on my school work and activities. Little time was given to reading the Bible and my attendance of the meetings was irregular. And as a major examination drew near, and for want of time to prepare for it, I had stopped going to the meetings. Having passed the examination, I went for a further stage of study at a college. Over there, I met two members of the Mission, who persuaded me to join them in their Bible study in another member's house, which I did but I went not to the meetings. They asked me the reason for not being present on Sunday meetings. I made excuses.

After I left college, I took a job in an accounting firm. During the first year in that company, I was miserable. I made a profession of the Christian religion before my work colleagues. The things taught from 'JSM' still remained in me but I compromised. I would not go to the cinema for a show, but the television was alright. As for music; country and sentimental music were alright but no, not the pop or rock

117

music. I kept worldly, short hair style, was taken away with worldly chit chat and jokes and kept worldly companionship. The love of the world was in my heart. In fact I broke many of the 'JSM' rules. But conscience was troubled. I could not give clear answers to some of the questions put forth by my colleagues. I was deeply miserable. Although I did enjoy the pleasures of this life for a season, it was for a season only. I soon found life totally meaningless and deep within I felt that great emptiness. I wished to die then but thought to myself, any suicidal move would stumble my colleagues. Now, nothing could satisfy me—not any worldly entertainment. I was nineteen then.

I went back to religion and desired to take it seriously. I kept consistent reading of the Bible. The lack of courage and pride kept me back from going to the Mission. For shame, that people should see me in this backslidden state. My younger sister, whom I had observed, had become serious and fervent in the Christian religion, had been to the Mission regularly for some months. One night, she approached me and spoke to me: encouraged me to come back. I decided to humble myself and went. Some at the Mission recognised me and were glad for me. I was encouraged. It happened, at that time, the Mission property was to be taken away by the authorities, and we had not many months to hold our meetings in the premises. My sister and I went to as many meetings as we possibly could. I thought I was revived. I read the Bible more carefully and found myself able to pray in the meetings. I went house to house tracting and desired much to be at the meetings.

In 1984 I thought I was called into full-time service. When I read the scriptures, passages, I thought then, seem to speak to me, to call me aside to serve the Lord, and messages which I heard from the meetings seemed to confirm it. I sought counsel. I was encouraged into it by one of the 'pastors' of the

Mission, besides the leader of my group, and also by a missioner. My heart was set on doing it; to leave my job and join the Mission. But I was fearful of the consequences to be faced with my parents. When I broke the news to my mother, she was shocked and surprised. My father objected to the whole idea and was very grieved when I actually did it.

I was guided by a missioner for a time, I had much time on my hands. Honestly, I was quite lost. I did not know what to do. My quiet time stretched longer in the morning. I spent most of the day reading the scriptures but did find, most of the time, that my reading was dry. My prayers were with much crying often, feeling the absence of God's presence. I had wanted to serve the Lord and please him but found his face hid from me. A voice sounded in my heart—what of your past sins! I felt his wrath gone forth against me in that the heavens were as brass. I cried to him for mercy but felt that he would not hear me because of all my iniquities. I wished I could go back in time to put things right.

Sometimes, I sat in my room for an hour or more staring blankly onto the wall and the ceiling, in much despair. But I hid my condition from the missioner, the 'pastor' and members in the Mission. I kept up tracting, visiting and accompanying the missioner to places and Bible studies at times. I kept myself occupied with reading books on prayer, devotion, revivals, and so on. I felt tried, and thought maybe I should go to a Bible college to be taught and trained to become a missioner. I think I would have if I had been sent.

I was quite disappointed when I did not receive any monetary support from the Mission as most of the full-timers and missioners had. I had given all that I had to the Mission. I felt very bitter, and murmurings were in my heart when I was, at times, left with no money for food or transport expenses. Then afterwards, I would condemn myself for feeling thus and for such thoughts. So I gave tuition to earn my keep.

A trip to Kuala Lumpur and Ipoh was organised in the year 1984 and I was to go to evangelise to the Malays because I knew their language. So I went and stayed in Kuala Lumpur at the Mission premises for a month. I was in much fear, feeling my incapability to help in any way to the work in Kuala Lumpur. And I was still troubled with the guilt of my sins unpardoned. Each time, to feel that I may pray aright to God, I made a confession of my sins. But there were times I felt my sins to be so dark, so grievous in the sight of God, that they could not be pardoned. I remember, in one overnight prayer meeting, in Kuala Lumpur, in the midst of my earnest cry and weeping because of my sins, these words came to me: Daughter, be of good cheer, thy sins be forgiven thee. I ceased from my crying, and lifted myself up from the posture of prayer. I think I never felt such a peace in my heart and my heart was filled with joy. I could not rest that night; pondering and wondering at those words.

In that same year, in December 1984, in Penang, there was to be a conference. And I learnt that a guest speaker from England was to address us in the evening meetings. I did not think much about it but, on the contrary, was wary of him because of some negative remarks the 'pastor', the missioner, and some others had made on him. But when I first heard him speak, and at the end of his first address, I said within my heart—never man spake like this man. I longed to hear him speak and looked forward to every evening.

I pondered much about this man, Mr. John Metcalfe, and the things which he spoke. In fact, I did not, at first, even know how his name was spelt. To me, he was a great speaker, and a very spiritual pastor of a church in England, and there should be, as I felt, that distance to be kept. But I found that he was also kind, gentle and considerate. He spoke to us freely and gave help when counsel was sought from him. I tried to grasp and retain every word he spoke.

In his first address, from I Thessalonians chapter 1, one question he asked before all of us remained in my heart. That was, Do we answer to the church as it is in God the Father and in the Lord Jesus Christ? I could not answer that question positively for I felt that in the light of that which Mr. Metcalfe brought forth of her characteristics, we did not measure to it. I doubted my salvation also. I was much encouraged from the words in his address from Psalm 11. They brought hope in his word.

I was delighted to know that later he would come to Singapore to address us. Though I could not fully understand or grasp all that the servant of the Lord spoke, at that time, there were other simple and plain issues which remained and troubled my heart and conscience. Issues such as the headship of Christ, and the distinction to be observed between men and women in the church. I became aware of the apostolic ordinance of the covering of the head of the woman when she prays or prophesies, which we did not observe or keep; of the apostle not suffering women to speak in the church, which we did, both in our Missions, and in the full-time service. I went back home and pondered upon the words. But I did not want to pursue further into the matters, so I cast aside all questions.

However, I did not have any rest, and in Mr. Metcalfe's last address in Singapore from Psalm 133, the words came with power and I was convicted in my heart. The words were so plain and clear, speaking to our states and conditions, one could not make them out to be of other meaning, nor find excuses. But to my grief, the leaders of the Mission, and many who had heard these words, refused to obey the word of God, which they claim they loved, boasting of being such fundamentalists in practice. Instead, they spoke evil of Mr. Metcalfe after he returned to England. A number of us left the Mission, seeing the impossibility to continue except the whole system be discarded and begin again with obedience to the word of God.

As I recall these things that have happened, I am thankful to the LORD for his mercy and the deliverance granted from the net of this legal system and its entangling errors. Though I had thought that I would stay in the Mission and serve therein for the rest of my life and had always thought their teachings to be right, yet to turn from this system of works and to take the step of obeying God's word by faith alone, I know it to be possible only by his grace and strength. And at that point of time, I felt as if all that I have trusted in and built upon was being crushed and destroyed and that there was no standing ground any more.

Mr. Metcalfe had to return to England for the unfinished work of writing the Hymns of the New Testament, and we hoped that he would be back shortly in the same year. Meantime, a former 'pastor' from the Mission led us in the group. After a while, I found a job.

During that time, I was under deep conviction of my sins and sinful state. My past sins were brought to my remembrance again and I was tormented in my mind, that they had not been forgiven. I asked, What shall I do? I also found myself sinning and continually sinning, in every hour that I was awake. I found myself sinning with my heart, with my mind, with my mouth and with my deeds. I was unable to put forth a good or a right thought. All manner of uncleanness and filthiness rose in my thoughts. It was with much regret that I ever did fill my mind with the filth and corruption from the television and worldly books, for these things came back to my mind and I found no strength not to remember or think of them. Besides, my heart did delight in them. I groaned over the state of my heart; wishing that I could really have a heart transplant. 'For out of the heart proceed evil thoughts, murders, adulteries, fornications, thefts, false witness, blasphemies.'

I discovered my heart to be deceitful above all things and desperately wicked. And worse, I had white-washed my true state with religion. I had made clean the outside by going to church, reading the Bible, praying, doing 'good' to others, helping the poor and abstaining from worldly entertainment but, inside, the heart was unclean, insincere, untrue, impure, worldly, ungodly, which appeared not to man. Every motive, every desire, and every deed done were from self-interest. The desire for man to think one to be saintly, religious, good and among Christians, as someone spiritual and zealous. Each time, when I would sneer or think ill of a drug addict, or a murderer, or a thief, or an harlot, my heart would be smitten as I remember the words of the Pharisee: God, I thank thee that I am not as other men are. But I was as other men are, if not worse, because of my hypocrisy and dishonesty.

I heard as if the Lord did say to me; I know you, that you have not the love of God in you. I opened not my mouth as far as possible, for I would condemn myself for the words that came forth. The more I sought to do good, the more evil was present with me. It was as if God had placed a large mirror before me, only this time it was for the inward man. And I saw my true state and was horrified by it. I was in a bitter and peevish spirit. I cursed the day I was born and wished that I had never been born. I desired to end my life and would have, were it not, I believe now, for the mercies of the Lord that prevented me. For at each try, the fear of death and the judgment ahead seized me.

My eyes were sore from weeping, I would go to bed as early as I could and make myself sleep, for then I would not be conscious for a while. Each day was a dread. I spoke to no one except for a sister, who had helped me and encouraged me to wait and hope. My work colleagues looked upon me with strangeness. I hardly spoke a word to them except about work. I had not gone to the meetings held by the former missioner, except on the first days and certain evenings when I was virtually forced to go. For I found this man brought more darkness and confusion upon my mind. He knew not nor could understand my state. He blamed a few others for their influence over me, hence bringing me into such a 'morbid' state as they called it.

One of them, a former missioner from 'JSM', came to visit me and counselled me to walk according to the word of God and not experiences or feelings. But I found the Psalms, the language of the psalmist, spoke to my heart. Though I may not have gone through the depth of the experience the psalmist had, that he should pray or cry thus, yet I could agree with the psalmist. I knew, in some measure, what he was talking about. And I found reading the Psalms such a delight and comfort to my soul. I read and re-read time and again the Psalms like Psalm 42, 38, 88, 142 and 143.

Mr. Metcalfe's letter on the 19th April, 1985, in reply to my letter to him, brought me hope and to wait upon the Lord. I was astonished at the contents of the letter. For I knew not that what was happening to me was the work of God. In my unbelief I said, How could this disgusting and contemptible creature be a child of God?

I was overjoyed when Mr. Metcalfe came back to Singapore in July 1985. And in his first address from Titus chapter 2, verse 11, my unbelief and hardness of heart were broken. As the truth of God's salvation was opened up, I was glad to behold the salvation which God the Father had purposed, outwrought by his Son, without us having the need to do anything, and not only so but that the Holy Ghost should come to bring this salvation into our hearts. And I believed.

The grace of God that bringeth salvation had appeared unto me. His love, the love of God, my Saviour, for me, over-whelmed my heart. My eyes were a fountain of tears, weeping for joy and relief. Truly it was renewal to my soul. He heals the broken-hearted and binds their wounds. I rejoiced with joy unspeakable and full of glory. There was a deep peace in my heart and my soul was brought into rest. His longsuffering is salvation. He hears the groanings of the prisoners and the sighs of the poor and needy.

I am thankful that God did send his servant, Mr. Metcalfe, into our midst at Penang and Singapore, that the true gospel of our Lord Jesus Christ should be preached unto us. And also that we have been taught the precious doctrine of Christ and been brought under this ministry, which is not a ministry of condemnation but of free justification by grace, of life and of the Spirit.

Blessed be God, which hath not turned away my prayer, nor his mercy from me.

Cindy Lee

A Testimony from
The Saints

Penang
December, 1988

Beloved Minister,

Though in the midst of manifold afflictions and trials, with the burden of the churches daily upon thee, with the responsibility of the work at the Trust, not forgetting thy wholehearted service in penning down Revealed truths, thou hast travailed much in prayer daily on our behalf that Christ may be formed in us. We are ever so grateful—beyond words! Also we have been mightily blessed through the hearing of the tapes and take this opportunity to thank thee for not having shunned to declare the whole counsel of God unto us. O may the LORD who made heaven and earth bless thee out of Zion (Psalm 134:3), and prosper thy health and extend thy life to bring forth much fruit unto his glory.

Your children in the faith,
Bethany and Bethphage

Penang
14th March, 1989

Dearly beloved Mr. Metcalfe,

We give thanks to him who is the Most High, whose throne is established in justice and judgment, and do rejoice exceedingly at the great deliverance he had granted thee, his servant.

O, may God the Father make thy pathway plain and grant the desires of thy heart, for the going forth of the gospel that many of his elect (even as we have been) be brought under this God-sent, powerful and effectual ministry which he had committed to thee.

We are indeed overwhelmed with gratitude to thee, for all thy instructions in righteousness, admonitions, rebukes, reproofs and exhortations that have accompanied the faithful preaching of the gospel. Thou hast nourished us even as a nurse nourishes a babe, travailing in prayer that Christ be formed in us. We give thanks to thee for thy longsuffering and forbearance towards us, suffering the loss of all things for the gospel and the elect's sake, ever enlarged in heart, spending and being spent for us.

Thank you once again, Mr. Metcalfe.

Your children in the faith,
All at Bethphage and Bethany

A TESTIMONY FROM THE SAINTS GATHERED
IN SINGAPORE AND PENANG, AFTER THE
MESSAGES 'GROWING IN GRACE'

PERTUBUHAN DEWAN MESYUARAT BETHPHAGE,
PULAU PINANG,
31ST MAY TO 3RD JUNE 1990

Dearly beloved Mr. Metcalfe,

We thank thee for thy great love and care for and patience with us that as a nurse cherisheth and nourisheth her children, so hast thou fed us with the sincere milk of the word that we may grow thereby.

We thank thee when at times we were sickly, thou prayed for us, brought us by faith to him who is the Life and took great pains to nourish us to health. Indeed, we thank thee for travailing thus that Christ should be formed in us.

As infants who could repay nought for all the love and care received, we could but thank God for putting thee into the ministry and us under thy ministry, desiring the Lord to open effectual doors of utterance to thee to prophesy again before many peoples, and nations, and tongues, and kings.

As for us, we will arise in faith and joy and press forward, trusting in the over-abounding grace and provision for growth from our heavenly Father through Jesus Christ our Lord, to whom be praise and glory both now and ever. Amen.

Thy little children in the Gospel (Gal. 4:19)

at Bethany Meeting Hall, Singapore;
and at Bethphage Meeting Hall, Penang

Bethphage Meeting Hall,
Penang
September, 1990

Our beloved Mr. Metcalfe,

We give thanks always unto God our Father and Jesus Christ our Lord for the ministry and grace which thou hast received from the everlasting God our Saviour.

We thank thee for constantly, in faith and love and with much longsuffering, putting us in remembrance of the things which be for his glory and honour.

O that the Lord of the harvest would send thee forth with the gospel of peace in the demonstration and power of the Holy Ghost to glorify Christ through the calling and gathering of his elect blood-covenanted people.

The Lord do so and more also for his great name's sake. May it be according to thy faith, and even to ours also though small it be as a mustard seed.

Thy children in the gospel,
sanctified by God the Father
and preserved in Jesus Christ.

A Letter from
Sie Siok Hui

Singapore
19th June, 1990

Dearly beloved Mr. Metcalfe,

This is written specially to thank you for the book 'The Church: What is it?' I have just finished reading it this morning. It is incredible how much of the truth has never been heard preached or written in our own day. My soul is speechless to enter into such divine mystery. The sound exposition shines as glittering gems: all the while in the Holy Bible, yet so blind am I that I have seen none of these things. How glorious the work of Christ in the building of the ecclesia! How filthy, how vile, how blind the works of man in religion.

There is so much to assimilate, so much to answer to. I was filled with much awe and truly believe with my whole heart that behind this book is the mighty moving of the Holy Ghost.

I know I have grieved you much this time. In fact, from the beginning when you were saddened because truth seemed to play so little part in the experience of us all, I was convicted of my own state. Throughout this time, I examine myself to see if I be in the faith. I embrace the precious truth concerning election, and that all is of grace, by the faith of Christ, and not by works. But I came short of the understanding, or the penetration of the doctrine of justification by faith. Nor can I fully apprehend the concept of righteousness.

When you spoke, to those of us who gathered in your apartment, of the obedience of Christ that brought forth everlasting righteousness, for the first time, some light dawned into my soul.

I was cut to the heart especially by the first message 'Growth in Grace', when you uncover why there is no growth—no faith, no hope, no love.

On another occasion, the last evening before David left, when Miss Ang, Suzanne, David, and I were up in your apartment, you asked me how to honour Christ, and I said in the heart. You said it was right, for the Plymouth Brethren err in that they talk of an objective Christ and his works outwardly, but not the indwelling of Christ, Christ in you, the hope of glory. I felt I was described—for my heart seemed so dead and hardened.

How true it is that I live a superficial life, skimming only the surface, conforming to outward appearance, but so worldly and ungodly at heart. Truly when I examine myself and my religion the last few years, I shudder. O that I may not be found as the foolish virgins without oil in the vessel.

There were times in these weeks that I despaired. But unto me has been given to hear the gospel, the doctrine of Christ. And I believe and do receive. Therefore I have much to give thanks and to praise our great God for his goodness to the children of men.

There is much I need to bring under. When I think of how many times I failed, my heart sank. But Christ has wrought the victory. Faith is against nature. The old man has been crucified. The cross must be carried daily. Please pray for me.

Please do not feel that what you say to me is not taken in. If I did not speak in response, it is really because I have nothing to say, save to repent before God, and to plead for grace to bring this vile self under subjection.

I do appreciate deeply all your unceasing labour, teaching and warning every one of us continually. I know I have tried your patience greatly and have let you down. If I were to say, from henceforth I would not do so, or I would amend myself, I fear less I fall under the yoke of bondage.

I can only quote the psalmist in Psalm 119:57-60. 'Thou art my portion, O Lord: I have said that I would keep thy words. I entreated thy favour with my whole heart: be merciful unto me according to thy word. I thought on my ways, and turned my feet unto thy testimonies. I made haste, and delayed not to keep thy commandments.'

Thank you very very much. I can never thank you enough for all that you have done for us, for me.

May the Lord grant that we would respond with vision to the truths preached unto us, and that the spirit of the bride in the ecclesia would answer to the Bridegroom, even to gather together in one visible unity in every locality, together throughout the world, with all saints throughout the age and say unto him 'Even so, come, Lord Jesus'.

Your daughter, begotten by the gospel,

Siok Hui

The Conversion of
David Khor Nyak Hiong

Singapore

June, 1990

Dear Mr. Metcalfe,

As you requested my testimony, that I should put down in writing all that I went through and felt when I was shut up from man unto faith in Jesus Christ our Lord, I do so with joy yet trembling lest I should omit anything that is to his glory.

Behold the exceeding goodness of our God, his graciousness, mercy and longsuffering toward one such as I who was so hardened and so slow of heart to believe. I thank the LORD that though I could not and would not believe for so long, he cannot and did not deny himself but overcame all my unbelief and granted me to obtain like precious faith with his elect people. Thanks be to our LORD for he is good: for his mercy endureth for ever. Praise be to our God who is mighty to save, redeem and gather his people.

Before you came to preach in Penang in December 1984, I had been formally in the Christian religion for over a decade. Many outward reformations I made and my manner of life was commendable in the sight of many. However I knew within my soul that all was empty: that I had sinned, that I had no forgiveness written in my heart, and that no matter how I tried to restrain myself I could not stop sinning. I knew truly that the only way I could stop sinning was to die. Yet I feared to die, for in such a case I knew not how I should stand in the day of judgment. I prayed for forgiveness but felt nothing at all. I dared not tell anyone of this for fear that others would discover my true state. I alternated between labourings to better myself to please God and despair under these convictions.

Many times, I just could not keep up with the front any longer, nor with the stated or unstated 'dos and don'ts' of a more 'fundamental' Christianity. I felt so out of place amidst the apparently fervent, zealous and religious 'brethren'. I often 'backslid'. During these times, I tried to enjoy the world and forget God but thanks be to God, he would not let me. I tried joining other 'churches', more liberal and less demanding. These seemed carefree, joyful and more loving, but I found no solution to my soul troubles and in my heart I could not wholly join myself to them. Finally, after years of wandering to and fro, I went back to the original 'church'. I soon made an impression and was even given certain responsibilities but I could not match their fleshly fervency and legal rectitude and I blamed myself and tried in vain to measure up to them.

It was with this 'church', at a certain conference, that I first heard you preach. I was particularly struck when you described the arrows of conviction in the heart of the sinner and the LORD's deliverance. O how I longed to be delivered, though my convictions were not as acute as described.

I marvelled at certain others in the meetings who rejoiced so greatly at hearing the preaching. I envied their joy. I remembered trying to pay greater attention, fearing to leave out anything in thy preaching that might afford me joy. I heard what they heard, this I found out by comparing with them later. The only thing I felt was at most an intellectual assent to what was preached. So I tried to work myself up but did not succeed much. I then managed to put on quite a convincing show of receiving the word and of outward joy. In fact, it was only after conversion that I found this to be what is called religion before man, always comparing oneself with others, caring for what others think, and not realising that one's hearing is before God only and that it is he that prepares the heart.

Afterwards, you remained in Malaysia and then came preaching and teaching in Singapore for about two weeks. Then troubles brewed. After you left, I saw those who invited you to preach, who praised you so fulsomely earlier, and even more rejoiced at your preaching, now turned against you in your absence, finding fault with your doctrine (though they hardly knew the word doctrine before you came) and character. Those who knew the spirit and truth of the things preached by you went out from them. One of their 'reverends' who was ever at odd with his own kind seized the opportunity and used your good name to lead these few saints together with his own disciples. I was perplexed for I knew this man and my soul had felt no peace under his 'legal' ministry. In my confusion, I knew not what to do, only felt disgust at the religious systems of man, full of vanity and self-seeking. I left all, quite frustrated. In despair, I felt like resigning myself to the world but could not both by the mercy of God, and by his exposing the world in I John 2:15-17.

I tried to seek God alone. On Sundays, I went to a public park to read and pray. I cried to God in my confusion. At times, I felt so lonely that I could just join those gathered with the ex 'reverend' but my conscience forbad me. How I ever went through this period I do not know, save only by the grace and goodness of my God.

There was an incident during this time that lifted me up a little. I remembered reading on one such Sunday about the Canaanitish woman who came to Jesus, humbled herself, persisted in faith and got an answer from the Lord though she was rejected at the first. This encouraged me considerably to wait on though it seemed then that the Lord could not be reached, cry as I might.

In the middle of 1985, I was informed that you had returned to preach again in Singapore, this time at the request of some others. The saints had come together and would be attending your ministry. One of these invited me and I deliberated much on the matter up to the very day of the meeting. I was late that first meeting. Why I attended it when I had kept away from the others, I knew not. I have searched hard to recall the cause but to no avail. I only knew that whatever moved me to do so was absolutely not to my credit. It could only be by the everlasting mercies of my God. However, I attended the meeting warily as I did not want to get hurt again. I kept aloof at the beginning and examined carefully, not as the Bereans did, but, alas, with a censorious and critical mind, all that was preached.

It was after quite a while and only after much prompting from certain others in the meeting that I went for the prayer and fellowship meeting at your own rented apartment. I believe it was the first meeting I had there that you asked me about conversion. I envied the others who could answer you with such confidence that they were saved. I could not. My recent readings in the gospel of John had troubled me. For I read of many who believed in his name and yet Jesus did not commit himself to them (2:23-25) and of those even called disciples, who believed and yet went away (6:66). What then was 'believing'? What was the difference between the believing in 2:11 and that in 2:23? Of which type was my 'believing'? How could I tell? So I could only say I did not know whether I was saved but that I was waiting on God. I thought you would be shocked at my doubting reply. Instead you encouraged me to wait on. Your words surprised me as I believed most others would try to assure me from scriptures.

After a few months, you went back to England to settle some affairs. It was only much later that I found out that certain wolves in sheep's clothing in the congregation there had conspired even with those of your own household, rising up in your absence to bring forth false accusations against you. You went back to clear your name and set matters right. The false accusers all fled from you, none would face you, so the Lord gave the victory, and you strengthened the saints and comforted the assembly. The few who went out into the darkness were soon scattered to the four winds, either falling away, or going back to what they had once left, as the sow to her wallowing in the mire, or the dog to his vomit (II Pet. 2:21-22).

The congregation in Singapore was not spared the rage of the enemy. Satan entered into the hearts of the two who had invited you and they also stood up in a meeting in your absence saying all manner of evil against you. We later learned that they had secretly communicated and conspired with the apostates in England. I was stunned. For in my heart I could never believe these false accusations, for I felt and knew the manner and spirit with which you preached. Because in my own experience, 'Never man spake like this man'.

But the wicked one worked through my natural suspicions and carnal reasonings and pointed me to certain religious men whose life and preaching did not agree. I was corrupted and weakened. I knew not then as I do now your devout and holy manner of life, coupled with the evident blamelessness of your conversation. In my foolishness I brought these trials upon myself, because I would keep aloof from you all this while. Then, however, I became angry at myself for not staying alone, and to a certain extent even angry at God for letting such trials come and doubts arise time and again.

What a beast I was as I look back! Did not the scriptures testify that the children of the flesh shall persecute the children of the promise, and that the apostles in the new testament times and even Jesus himself suffered like things from the religious in their days? 'On their part he is evil spoken of but on your part he is glorified.' For this uncontrollable rage of the enemy, the actual *manifestation* of Satan, both in England and Singapore, in such terrible enmity, in fact provided the clearest evidence and corroboration of a true ministry sent from God.

However, I knew not these truths then by experience, and my steps faltered under the lies and wiles of the wicked one. It was only by God's own teaching that I was brought to know that persecutions and false speakings are inevitably consequential upon the preaching of the true gospel of Christ. Still, weak and foolish as I was, by the grace of God, though I did not yet fully understand, I began slowly to realise these things, for my soul testified to the truth both of the way you lived among us, and of the Holy Ghost upon your preaching. Besides this the evil one gave himself away, even to me, by the devilish uncontrol of the accusers' rage and lies. I was by these observations persuaded and kept with the saints.

When these things happened in Singapore, you rushed back from England to strengthen us in the faith. Then these liars shrunk away and dared not look you in the eye, nor face you, to repeat their vile inventions in your presence! No, not one of them. Their own conscience condemned them. Then you, knowing that the same wicked rage would not be spared from the saints in Penang, went to strengthen their faith also. After which you returned to us and after much exhortation and encouragement, left for England once again to face yet another series of trials, as the enemies of the gospel went about to destroy the work of God in both the Meeting and the Trust. After you left, the enemies here told lies to the Authority so that your work permit would be revoked, and in that way you could be prevented from returning to labour for Christ in Singapore.

In the midst of all these troubles, the Lord was exceedingly gracious to grant us, in June 1986, a more permanent meeting-place instead of meeting at a public conference room. Thus, we were enabled to meet more often and encouraged one another.

About a month before the Penang meetings in December 1986, I had occasional sharp pain near the heart. And I feared dying, for I knew not where I stood before God. I had in the previous few months assumed that the Lord had answered my waiting, but I confess that this was complacency, for now I found neither assurance nor peace within, because of the fear of death.

At the meeting in Penang, I even stood up to exhort others and tried to comfort another. I agreed with what you preached and learnt many things from reading the scriptures. I regarded such progress as 'revelations' and rejoiced. Secret pride crept into my heart and mind.

When you called all of us up to your apartment the Saturday that we were leaving I felt something was wrong but did not think there was any problem with me. After opening the state of heart in others, exhorting them, I was shocked when you turned to me and said, 'David, you have no faith'. This struck at my heart: I was utterly convicted. For I knew that I had never once been sure or had assurance that I had believed in the Lord, that I had faith, or that he had saved me. I felt lost and could only ask, 'What must I do?' You replied to wait still upon the Lord, and recounted my first talk with you in your apartment at Taman Serasi, Singapore, in 1985. You closed with prayer and interceded for us. I broke down and wept bitterly.

Yet how the flesh, fully alive, began working immediately. I thought the Lord would have respect to my cryings. I thought to be as Jacob not letting him go till he blessed me. I really thought I could get God to answer me there and then. Alas, miserable, presumptuous sinner, I got no reply. All that I had done crumbled, all that scriptural knowledge, all my cherished revelations availed nothing. What was the use of all these things, if I could not find Christ?

I left your place ashamed and shattered. About an hour later, you came over to Jalan Azyze, where we were staying, to speak with certain others. Before leaving, you came to me and kindly encouraged me to wait still upon God, exhorting me not to show sadness in my countenance, lest I should discourage the younger ones. You then came with us to see us off at the station.

On the coach back, I was led almost immediately to Psalm 130. Indeed, 'if thou, LORD, shouldest mark iniquities, O Lord, who shall stand? But there is forgiveness with thee that thou mayest be feared.' My soul cried to the LORD for mercy and I took comfort that 'with the LORD there is mercy, and with him there is plenteous redemption.'

When the coach stopped for dinner, I was ashamed and did not want to sit with the rest. But they invited me over and showed me kindness. When we reached Singapore, at the meeting-place, I found that you had told the rest to treat me still as a brother. I was touched.

The first half of the year 1987 was a trying period of waiting. At various times, in your absence, certain left the meeting, and I had to 'take' the meetings, being the more 'elderly' brother. I did not want this, but for the sake of the rest, I did it, even whilst crying to the Lord for salvation. Many times I shrank from praying in the meetings. But if I prayed not I feared discouraging others. Yet how could one such as I pray?

Many times, my heart failed me, and I wanted to leave, but the LORD graciously encouraged me from such scriptures as Psalm 130, Psalm 119:169-176, Psalm 25, Psalm 43, Psalm 51 and Psalm 143, and I sang again and again these passages from 'The Psalms of the Old Testament', in which you set down so faithfully the Psalms into metrical verses for singing. How comforting and seemly to sing from the scripture itself, from psalms and hymns and spiritual songs.

Now, as I look back, I can only thank the LORD that he who called me to wait on him also gave the strength to endure until he appeared to my soul. Indeed he upheld me in my waiting with his right hand, as said David, 'In waiting I waited upon the LORD.'

There were two occasions, months apart, when I really had no strength to go on, when I was exceedingly overwhelmed because of my sins. On both occasions, Psalm 38 was impressed deeply upon my soul, so that I used to stay back after the meetings, when I could contain myself no longer, weeping bitterly before the LORD. I pleaded for mercy, and brought his words in Romans 10:13 before him.

It was sometime between these two occasions that I wrote to you, saying how I felt like an Achan in the camp, that I was ready to halt. You replied comfortingly and showed me that I was in the footsteps of the flock, and that neither goat nor hypocrite ever once experienced such dealings. You again encouraged me to wait on assuring me that at his time appointed the LORD would appear to my salvation. I am so thankful for this letter, which the Spirit used to strengthen me, that I might continue to seek the light of his countenance who had whispered long ago to my soul 'Seek ye my face', and I had replied 'Thy face, LORD, will I seek'.

In the latter half of 1987, providentially, we started replaying the tape messages of your preaching in chronological order. I had heard these messages before with the outward ears. But now, when the Lord himself unstopped my ears, he likewise opened my heart to attend to the things which you had said: O, what an entrance of faith! what joy to hear that salvation belongeth unto God and to him only. That he had chosen a people unto salvation in Christ from before the foundation of the world. That he alone can turn these sinners to himself and that he does so when they themselves find by experience that they cannot turn themselves.

How long the lesson takes! The lesson that he by the Spirit awakens, alarms, and convicts sinners, quickening them, and bringing them to faith in Jesus Christ. That, though they be ungodly, still, God is just to justify them freely by his grace through the redemption that is in Christ Jesus, even when there is as yet not a single interior change in them. What a justification by faith, and what a wonderful atoning basis for it! That this righteousness, imputed without works, is a divine righteousness! That salvation is outside of oneself, found in another, even Jesus, who shall save his people from their sins. How that salvation is all wrought at the cross, all in the blood of Christ, all freely by grace through faith alone, and that it is all of God to open the ear, enlarge the heart, and bring to faith in Christ.

How these things rejoiced my weary soul, long crushed under sin and the law. For the first time, I gladly received your words. 'Ah, but are you elect?' came that haunting voice of the tempter. Whether so or not, I could not but praise God, for I both felt and knew that 'He is great and greatly to be praised.' His works declared his greatness and his glory eclipsed my salvation. If I perished, I perished, but I would praise him for his creation, his works in Christ, his love to his saints, and for his longsuffering to such a beast as I.

When the December 1987 Penang meetings drew nigh, somehow I dreaded to go. But I thought, this is the flesh: what care I for its feelings? The flesh never will profit anything. I remembered being comforted by Hebrews 12:5-11. Still, I besought the LORD not to rebuke me, who had waited so long upon him, no, not in wrath, for who can stand the power of his anger?

The Lord comforted me, and, in preparing for the readings from Ruth, I was overwhelmed by his grace and mercy toward me. My heart melted and gave thanks when I read Ruth 2:10, and I said with Ruth, 'Why have I found grace in thine eyes, that thou shouldest take knowledge of me, seeing I am a stranger?'

But Satan accused me, as he did so often during that year, of my many sins, filthiness, and corruption, and especially of my carnality, always full of worldly reasonings, and that the Lord would never love such a one as I. I could reply nothing, but only turn in my soul looking to the Lord for mercy.

From the very first day in Penang, the Lord comforted me exceedingly, speaking to my soul from Ezekiel 16:1-14, so that my heart melted at his love and goodness to me.

The remaining days were truly days of heaven on earth. Thy preachings from Psalms and Revelation were mightily brought home with the anointing and power of the Holy Ghost. The Lord was greatly exalted, and I saw no man save Jesus only. My heart rejoiced greatly and I praised the great God with his saints. (No man I ever knew glorified Christ as you did then, and, I bear witness, as you still do.)

I worshipped in awe at the grand counsel of the Lord God that he has purposed two seeds in the earth, that the goats and the sheep have been determined from eternity and shall be irrevocably separated at the day of judgment. Yea, he would have mercy on whom he would have mercy and whom he would he would harden. Whether vessels of mercy or vessels of wrath, all are ordained for his glory! Amen and amen.

'Redemption is not for man's glory but for God's glory!' you proclaimed. My soul resounded whole-heartedly, and gladly I felt the 'Amens', as all angels, the twenty-four elders, and the living creatures bore record to the majesty and dominion of God our Saviour.

Yea, LORD, Let this thy grand doctrine be preached throughout the remaining age and thy awesomeness and glory be felt in the heart of every man, in every company, godly or otherwise. For who shall not fear thee, O Lord, and glorify thy name?

The readings from Ruth were exceedingly gracious and I felt to a great extent being led by the selfsame way as Ruth. But Satan accused me again that I was worse than Ruth, that I was totally carnal and worldly, full of schemings and pretences that if the Lord would save me, it would not have taken all these years. Thanks be to God, I truly believed the LORD that had chosen Jerusalem rebuked him. 'It is God that justifieth, who is he that condemneth?'

On the morning of the first day of 1988, during the prayer-meeting, the Spirit brought home with such power and comfort the verse in Hebrews 11:21, 'By faith Jacob when he was a dying ... worshipped, leaning upon the top of his staff.' Oh, the LORD's gracious dealings with Jacob. Though he was a schemer and supplanter, full of carnal wisdom, yet the LORD made him a worshipper decades later. My heart melted at his goodness and longsuffering towards me all these years and I thanked my God and Saviour, even the God of Jacob.

Again the next morning, at prayers, I was comforted by the Lord's assurance that in his great mercy he had forgiven me all my sins, even before there was any change in me. And that though I was so slow to believe this, he abideth faithful. Behold the marks in his hands and his side!

That evening on my way back to Singapore, an inexplicable sorrow crept into my soul, and Satan thereby brought forth his accusations to discourage me. But the LORD assured and comforted me from Isaiah 54 and especially verse 10, 'For the mountains shall depart, and the hills be removed;'—and they surely shall in the day of wrath—'but my kindness shall not depart from thee, neither shall the covenant of my peace be removed, saith the LORD that hath mercy on thee.' O what grace, what mercy, what a covenant of his peace!

Another immediate token of kindness granted me comforted my heart greatly when, a few days later, I was in the thick of my army training. It was a clear morning and there was a sudden light drizzle which lasted only a few minutes. Yet I saw the rainbow arched against the clear blue. Straightway I knew in my spirit it was the LORD's work, and the Spirit brought Isa. 54:10 and Rev. 4:3 to remembrance. My heart melted at the faithfulness of my LORD, that he really and truly loves me, and remembers me.

O blessed be the LORD that hath chosen Jerusalem, who loves his people with an everlasting love and who has wrought such a great salvation, even eternal redemption through Jesus Christ, to the praise of the glory of his grace.

In closing, I could not but recount two other gracious milestones the LORD afforded me in my pilgrimage and fight of faith.

The first was in June 1988, after the brethren's prayer-meeting. My faith wavered when I looked away from Jesus, and instead looked at the long spiritual journey ahead, not knowing how I could endure it. While on the bus back from that meeting, John 11:25-27 was brought to my soul with exceeding grace and power. That HE is the resurrection: and utterly dead as I was, I believed in him and lived! That HE is the life: now being quickened from deadness, I lived and believed that I should never die! 'Believest thou this?' My soul declared gladly, 'Yea, Lord: I believe. I believe that thou art the Christ, the Son of God.' Unspeakable joy flooded my soul and my mouth was filled with praises. I sang, yea, I sang praises to my Lord and my God.

The second was a most blessed time of communion with my Lord when he awoke me early on 27th December 1988. He granted me such humbling sweet meditations, from Hebrews 10, on the efficacy of his sacrifice, blood and priesthood.

After this, I was led to Numbers 16. And fear came upon my soul knowing that I had sinned against the LORD in not taking heed to thy ministry at the first, hearkening instead to the evil-speakers. The Lord searched out from the inner recesses of my heart, though once hidden to me, the traces of those lies. Yea, I have heard thy gospel and thy proclamation of Jesus Christ, seen thy manner of life, diligence, afflictions for the ministry's and the elect's sakes, thy spending and being spent for the saints. O why had I not stopped my ears at their lies! I trembled and begged the LORD for forgiveness. He spake to my soul, 'Fear not, arise'. And I obtained mercy because I did it ignorantly in unbelief. And I gave thanks for thy ministry, for being brought under it, and prayed the Lord to send thee forth to preach his glorious gospel to many peoples and all the more in these last days.

Melted at his great kindness and longsuffering with me, the Spirit then led me again to the epistle of Jude. He lifted up my eyes to behold that the eternal counsel of God shall surely stand despite what ungodly wicked men, fallen angels or devil can do against it. My heart was filled with praises and worship as my eyes were turned, as John's were, from the state of the churches to behold the only wise God our Saviour and to praise him *now*, above the waves of apostasy and worldly wickedness. To declare with Jude in the selfsame spirit:

'Now unto him that is able to keep you from falling, and to present you faultless before the presence of his glory with exceeding joy, to the only wise God our Saviour, be glory and majesty, dominion and power, both now and ever. Amen.' And Amen.

Begotten and kept by the power of God
through faith unto salvation,

David Khor

The Conversion of
Wong Woon Siew, A Schoolgirl

Singapore
29th December, 1988

Dear Mr. Metcalfe,

It's been a blessing meeting you. I really longed for those days when we were in Penang. Now, back in Singapore, I send you my testimony.

I had been trapped in an 'Evangelical' group for about six years. Young and zealous, I attended many of their meetings and activities. Many were fun-filled and attracted many youngsters. I was actually asking myself whether I'm saved when I was in that group. I approached those 'Sunday school teachers' and they assured me and I blindly followed. All along, I had thought that I was on the right track, safe and sound, feeling very complacent and self-righteous too. I had even tried converting people and worked for salvation. Oh! how foolish, deceitful and blinded I had been.

I want to thank God for showing me the true way. Truly, it's his mercy and grace that the truth be brought to me.

Even as I looked back, during the period when I attended both Bethany and the Presbyterian church, there was much confusion in me. Doubts and questions were in me. I was actually asking God 'why this and why that'. I was shaken, nothing to cling on to. It was during this period that I became aware that, even though having professed Christianity for six years, I knew nothing of God, of Jesus Christ, or of the Holy Spirit. My 'faith' was so shallow, and I realised that I had wasted those six years and how I've sinned against God. I felt the emptiness in my heart and realised what a hypocrite I had been. However, having pride and being unsure of myself and wanting to cling on to the 'old church', I did not confess to God, but deep in my heart, I knew that it was the truth that I had heard preached at Bethany.

I dragged on till I was at the meeting at Penang. From the first day of my arrival (19.12.88) I was very burdened. In my heart, I knew I was not saved, for the concept of 'salvation' with which I had been whitewashed was so different from that which I'd read in the tract named 'The Grace of God That Brings Salvation'. However, I did not want to tell anyone about the true state of my heart. I tried to hide, and even prayed in my heart that this burden would go off. But it didn't turn out so, moreover, the image of judgment day in which God separates the sheep and the goats came vividly to me. The heaviness in my heart was unbearable and I could not but approach one of the sisters and seek for counsel. I wept and confessed to God and asked for his mercy but I had doubts in me.

Mr. Metcalfe, it was after your preaching on the Parable of the Sower, and the ministry on 'stony hearts', that I called on God to take away all my unbelief, and all the stones in my heart, that he might sow his seed in good ground.

I thank God for this revelation, and I'm glad to confess that Jesus Christ is my Lord and Saviour. What joy I have in my heart to know this truth from God. He truly is, and the precious blood of Christ has cleansed me from all my unrighteousness and sins, and he has imputed righteousness to me. Not only that, Christ is risen and is seated at the right hand of God, having won victory over death. What a Saviour I have!

Truly, God is very merciful to me. His grace is so bountiful that no words can express my gratitude to him. This is the work that God has wrought in my heart. This is only the beginning of the pilgrimage. There's still a long way and, like a child, I yearn for spiritual milk from on high that I may grow in the grace of our Lord and Saviour Jesus Christ.

To God be the glory and honour for ever and ever! Amen.

In His love,

Wong Woon Siew

To: Wong Woon Siew   High Wycombe,
From: John Metcalfe   Bucks.

5th January, 1989

My dear daughter in Christ,

Grace be to you, mercy and peace, from God our Father
and the Lord Jesus Christ.

I know that now you will be sorely tried and tempted by the
enemy of your soul, and by the powers of darkness, to doubt
the work of God and his love for you personally in Christ, and
to feel that you cannot be pleasing to him. Nevertheless, he
has clothed you with righteousness not your own, freely given
to you as your own, and he has given to you his free Spirit,
and hence says 'Thou art all fair, my love'. And why should
he do such things, or utter such sayings, were it not for love?

Why should he love you? Not for anything in you, much less
for anything you have done. When he found you, he said 'Thy
birth and thy nativity is of the land of Canaan, thy father
was an Amorite, and thy mother a Hittite.' By saying this,
stating that your origins were of the filthiest, vilest, most
unclean, uncircumcised, idolatrous nations, he is telling you
that—in the interpretation thereof—you must cry and lament
what is no more than the truth: 'Behold, I was shapen in
iniquity: and in sin did my mother conceive me': that is from
the land of Canaan with a witness, and to have an Amorite
for a father, and a Hittite for a mother indeed, for 'the wicked
are estranged from the womb, they go astray as soon as they
be born'—especially in religion—'speaking lies'. Now, what
birth is it that is from Canaan, whose father is an Amorite,
and whose mother a Hittite, spiritually? The whole race of

mankind without exception, for, 'By one man sin entered into the world, and death by sin: and so death passed upon all men, for that all have sinned'; because, 'By one man's disobedience, many were made sinners.'

Then why should he love you? Because he had pity upon you, since you had nothing to plead, nothing to pay, knew nothing, were nothing, and could do nothing for yourself. He loved you because he pitied you, he pitied you because you were helpless, and 'None'—other—'eye pitied thee, to have compassion upon thee, but thou wast cast out in the open field, to the loathing of thy person, in the day that thou wast born. And when I passed by thee, and saw thee polluted in thine own blood, I said unto thee when thou wast in thy blood, Live; yea, I said unto thee when thou wast in thy blood, Live.' He loved you for causes of everlasting, unutterable, immeasurable, unfathomable love within himself, 'for his great love wherewith he loved us', saying to you, 'I have loved thee with an everlasting love.'

Don't question this, or reason about it, or relate it to others. Give thanks for it with all your heart always! Be sure it is because you are nothing, none other loved you, you have nothing to plead, you are empty and lost, that his bowels yearned over you with compassion, and out of a race of dead men, chose you out to live and glorify him and him alone, his mercy and his alone, to give all the praise to free grace, that you might show forth the merit and worth of a Saviour, even Jesus our Lord, manifesting the everlasting love of God to the destitute and worthless, to take them from the dunghill, and set them among princes. Thus, all the glory is his, as it is written, That no flesh should glory in his presence. 'He that glorieth, let him glory in the Lord.'

Lay aside all reasoning, put every doubt away. No matter what you feel, or when you feel it; no matter how dark it seems, or how low you sink: nothing can give a beginning and therefore nothing an end to the word which has been spoken to you 'I have loved thee with an everlasting love.' You did nothing; he did not love you because you asked him: he loved you before you were born, yea, before the world was. And, since that love is eternal, he will love you when the world is no more. 'Herein is love, not that we loved God, but that he loved us.' No cause in you: you neither asked for it, warranted it, deserved it, earned it or could keep it; there was nothing lovely in you to him, nothing desirable, to the contrary. Nevertheless, he chose to set his love upon you, and take you up, and bless you, and wash you, and justify you, and sanctify you by the blood of his own Son, and since he has done these things, he will never leave thee nor forsake thee.

Remember this when you are harassed, or down, or cannot find time to do this, or that, or think it all depends on you: your righteousness before God is by the blood of Christ, in heaven, outside of yourself, and is not and cannot be affected by what you feel on earth. It is an objective righteousness, not in you, but in Christ for you. This righteousness is an everlasting righteousness, wrought before you were born, reserved for you when Christ's blood was shed, and brought to you when he said to you, as you lay in filth, blood and corruption, 'Live'. Praise the LORD! Let us exalt his name together! Never forget: your standing is not what you are, but what Christ is outside you before God. Your righteousness is not in you but in his blood sprinkled before the throne in heaven. Then lift up your heart, rejoice greatly, O daughter of Zion, and praise the LORD at all times, my daughter, crying with a loud voice, 'I will bless the Lord, so long as I live.' And so says your devoted pastor and father in Christ, John Metcalfe. Amen and Amen.

> In the bonds of everlasting love,
> and the grace of our Lord Jesus Christ,
> John Metcalfe

Fruit that Remains

THESE converts, together with very many others of similar experience—whose testimonies for lack of space are not included—both in the Far East and in the U.K., have continued until this present day. This must be so: 'Herein is my Father glorified, that ye bear much fruit; so shall ye be my disciples.' And again, 'Ye have not chosen me, but I have chosen you, and ordained you, that ye should go and bring forth fruit, and that your fruit should remain: that whatsoever ye shall ask of the Father in my name, he may give it you.'

This is the ministry of the new testament. Such a ministry is marked by continual fruitfulness, by fruit that is gathered, and by fruit that remains. This appears in the ministry of all those sent by the Father and the Son, as he says, 'Every branch in me that beareth not fruit he taketh away: and every branch that beareth fruit, he purgeth it, that it may bring forth more fruit', John 15:2, as the psalmist declares, 'They shall still bring forth fruit in old age'. Of the reality and experience of this, the following, among many others, bear witness to this present day.

The Conversion of Martin Kelly

Rochdale
15th April, 1990

I was brought up in the Roman Catholic religion, and was taken by the hand every week to attend and hear the Mass.

151

Even as a small child I felt proud of myself for doing what I thought pleased God.

I can truly say of those early days that when I knew God, I glorified him not as God, neither was I thankful—and subsequently my life became a testimony to the inevitable consequence—I became vain in my imagination, and my foolish heart was darkened.

I remember however at times very powerful impressions upon me, and once, as I stood in the middle of the playing field at school—being then about thirteen years old—such a wind blew across the field as nearly knocked me over and I was filled with wonder and felt deep down, there is a God. And as the wind roared and rushed past me I felt such a conviction of God's existence.

But the LORD was not in the wind.

I went on in my own ways for years after this until the time of rebellion set in, and despising of all authority. As I matured, so the more dark and foolish I became.

Of course it's only now that I realise how foolish I was, but if someone had asked me at the time I would have professed myself to be wise; after all I believed in God, which I thought was an excellent thing to do and very commendable and I really looked with scorn on those that didn't.

Anyway, as I said, the time of self-assertion came and the casting off of the restraints of my parents who had brought me up very well. It was at this time that I left off going to Mass, feeling that everyone who attended were hypocrites, except me of course.

I began to hate the whole idea of organised religion and thought that God was far above all these empty ceremonies.

So, in my darkness, I began to seek God, being determined to know who he was and being convinced that he could be known personally. Although I was still in my sins at this time and knew next to nothing of my state before Almighty God, yet I felt such powerful desires to know him, and often I went out for long walks and my heart's cry was 'Oh that I knew where I might find him'.

Soon I began to feel an incredible distance between myself and God. I felt even then to be so far off. In spite of all that I read, much of which was theological darkness, and in spite of all that I did, I felt there was a great gulf fixed, and had this sense of complete emptiness. It felt so awful to see the wonders of the natural creation and yet to feel so far off from him who made all things and who upholds all things.

I began to despair; and I feel that no other book of scripture explained my feelings at that time better than the book of Ecclesiastes, where the vanity of all things is seen. I looked on the left and behold it was dark, I looked up, and behold confusion, I looked to the right, and behold vanity and vexation of spirit.

I saw myself to be infinitely small and totally worthless, and that the whole world, the whole universe, was just one big accident, and, though the words would never pass my lips, yet I thought in my heart with the fool 'There is no God'. How I came to feel it I don't know, but it got fast hold of me until I could see nothing but meaningless darkness and a real fear of death, without hope—without God.

I went on in this state, more or less, for years until I remember reading the words of Jesus 'He that cometh to me I shall in no wise cast out' and they seemed so beautiful to me. In all my experience up to this point, even though I had been brought up with the name of Jesus on my lips, I had never given any thought about him. It was always God out there at a distance, I never considered the name or the Person of Jesus. There was no beauty that I should desire him, he was despised and rejected of me, not realising that he was appointed of God to be the Head-stone of the corner.

At this time also I read that 'the Lord is risen indeed' and 'I am the way, the truth, and the life' and 'before Abraham was I AM' which showed to me his deity and that he was very God. I remember these truths breaking in upon me and I felt so full of joy at the very thought of them.

I remember sending off for some literature, and in a booklet enclosed was an exhortation to seek the Lord in prayer to forgive my sins. Immediately upon reading it I fell to my knees and begged God in the name of his Son Jesus Christ to forgive me for all my life of sin and I felt such a peace inside.

I feel the Lord in his condescension to me really touched my heart at that time and made me to feel how impossible it was that I could ever find him or know him by myself. I saw the crucifixion of Christ as the only way for a sinner to be justified in his sight, and really felt he had died for me.

Soon I began to ask the Lord which place he would have me to attend to worship him and I prayed that as he knew all things, he knew I wanted to please him because of his mercy to me. I was fully prepared to go anywhere he would indicate, and began to wander from denomination to denomination and lifting up my eyes to the Lord to look for some indication of the right way. At this point I began to read Mr. Metcalfe's books, wherein were some challenging statements about the reality of the work of God in a person's heart. I read 'The Strait Gate' and 'The Gospel of God', and I can say that I had never read it on this wise before. By these books the Lord brought me to question all his dealings with me, and to bring them to the light of his word.

I looked at myself and how, even after professing the name of Christ, I still seemed to fall into sin. I tried to fight against it but there it was. Now I began to feel something deeper than my sins, and I remember one night reading in my bible 'It is no more I that do it but sin that dwelleth in me' and I realised that there was that in me that affected all my best intentions and that all my righteousnesses were as filthy rags. I remember crying out to the Lord how hopeless I was.

I then got into a state that I can't well describe. I felt even darker than I had before being a Christian, which thing so confused me as I thought I should be getting better, but instead I seemed worse. Now I began to lose all hope of God's mercy because I felt, not only was I still sinful but I had presumed upon his grace. I remember praying at the time that the Lord wouldn't leave me to myself or suffer me to presume. Truly 'unless the LORD had been my help, my soul had almost dwelt in silence'. I thought I had better give up any profession of Christianity and that surely my lot was among foolish virgins and thorny ground hearers.

I remember, in this condition, walking from work to the bus stop to catch my bus home; everything seemed to contribute to the confusion and despair I felt—the bustling crowds, the noise of the traffic and the blue sky almost out of sight between the office blocks. As I took my seat on the bus, a person began to read his newspaper, which had a picture of part of the face of a murderer, with the headline 'This Evil Monster' and I really felt that there was no difference between me and him, I felt capable of anything. All the time I called upon the Lord for help, seeing no refuge in myself or in anything else.

At this time we had begun to receive tapes of Mr. Metcalfe's ministry, and though at times I felt risings of faith within, nothing could compare to the night when my wife and I listened to the word from Revelation 12:10 about the accuser of the brethren.

155

In the midst of these trials of mine the Lord was pleased to quicken my mother into life. Having long laboured to please God in the Roman Catholic religion by fastings and prayers, indulgences and rosaries, confessions, good works, and pilgrimages, she was set free as she searched the scriptures and found him of whom the prophets and apostles did speak. She read that the blood of Christ was that *alone* which redeems and justifies—at which point the light broke in upon her and melted her into tears.

A short while afterwards she was struck by the words of Jesus where he says 'Go, show thyself to the priest'. So the following Saturday being confessional day, she went, and was able to make a good confession, as she told the priest what had happened. The priest however warned her to be careful and not to turn away from the sacraments. But she knew in her heart that fifty odd years of taking sacraments hadn't revealed Christ to her soul, nor did they, nor could they, blot out one sin.

As for my wife, she was quickened after much fear of being eternally lost without Christ. The word of the Lord broke in upon her soul with such power as to cause her to fall on her knees in gratitude and thanksgiving, being lost in wonder, love and praise—the word which came as so fitting to her condition was 'Lo, I am with you alway, even unto the end of the world'. This word of the Lord's unconditional mercy was to be confirmed to her as we heard Mr. Metcalfe speak from Revelation 12:10. Which brings me back to that memorable evening.

No doubt we were both in heaviness through manifold temptations, no doubt we were full of unbelief and hardness of heart, no doubt we sat in darkness and the shadow of death; these things were true but as Mr. Metcalfe opened the scriptures about the Adversary and accuser of the brethren, and as he spoke about his accusations being accusations of law, and how he brings a child of God into confusion by showing us how we have failed and how unworthy we are; and as Mr. Metcalfe spoke of Joshua the high priest clothed in *filthy rags*! I felt, 'that's me'.

And as he spoke of Satan's cruel taunts as to our unfitness to serve God because of being defiled with sin, I felt 'yes yes, it's true it's true' and as he spoke of the subtle devices of Satan in getting us locked into looking at ourselves I felt 'Oh yes, it's me it's me, I am the man'; and as Mr. Metcalfe said, 'but the Lord's got an answer!' my heart leaped within me and as he said 'Election, that's God's answer!' 'The LORD rebuke thee, O Satan; even the LORD that hath chosen Jerusalem rebuke thee: is not this a brand plucked out of the fire?' I could hold it in no longer for at this my wife and myself broke down into tears of such joy and relief as I can never ever describe with words. I'd never felt the grace of God so manifest before.

What staggered me was that Joshua said nothing wilst all these accusations rolled on around him, he just stood there in his filthy rags—what could he say—what could I say? But what overwhelmed me was that the very condition which I felt would exclude one for ever was no hindrance to his almighty grace, that he should choose me, who had done nothing but sin.

It seemed as if the whole plan of salvation was set before me in a moment of time as I traced his wonderful election from eternity past, down into time at the coming of his Son, on through the cross where the purchase was made, and up into glory, with no might, power or dominion in heaven or earth able to stop or withstand his almighty grace.

Since that time the Lord has graciously led us, by the preaching of this gospel, to stand outside of the professing denominational structures. Not because we are anything or can do anything, but to wait upon the Lord to reveal his will to us.

Since that time I can say, by grace, that it's been my constant desire that the Lord would teach us his way and lead us in his truth, and show us his paths.

It's not been easy to come out of the general profession of Christianity, especially as we feel ourselves to be nothing. One is tempted with whispers of 'What do these feeble Jews?' but we are persuaded, notwithstanding all our feelings, that Christ is 'without the camp'. The Lord knows the way that we take and when he has tried us we shall come forth as gold.

We want to wait upon the Lord, trusting in him who promises to make crooked things straight, to make rough places smooth, to make darkness light, and to lead the blind by a way that they know not.

I can't close this account of the Lord's dealings and mercies without adding a word of testimony to the ministry of Mr. Metcalfe which came to us at such a seasonable time.

I can testify to the Lord really blessing the word to us under the preaching on the tapes, and can recall many memorable blessings such as 'I was glad when they said unto me ...' when we were encouraged by the consideration of the Lord delighting in his people coming before him and holding out their hands and saying 'Oh! let us go up into the house of the Lord'. Also the word 'Thou art Peter, and upon this rock I will build my church' which was instrumental in bringing us finally to stand clear outside the camp of denominationalism.

Also 'How shall a man be just with God', where the impossibility of man being just is set wonderfully against God's free salvation. And many, many more instances of the Lord helping us by this ministry could be cited: 'How amiable are thy tabernacles', 'Christ Jesus came into the world to save sinners', 'The marriage at Cana of Galilee', 'Light from heaven' and so on. What a privilege it is to be under a faithful gospel minister in these days.

Thanks be unto God for all his mercies, and may the Lord have all the praise and lead us on for his name's sake.

Martin Kelly

The Conversion of Paul Giles

Wolverhampton
April, 1990

To testify as to the Lord's dealings with me and how he has lead me by the Holy Spirit has been quite an exercise. It has been the subject of much prayer, to write down what is true and what is experienced of God, that no room should be given to conjecture, supposition or vanities. I pray and trust that what follows will be blessed by the Lord and that the Spirit of truth will guide my pen to write what will be of profit and joy to others.

I was born into a Roman Catholic tradition and educated for fourteen years, firstly, by Carmelite nuns and, lastly, by Marist brothers. I was to all intents and purposes a devout 'cradle' Catholic. By the time I was eighteen I had cast off this profession as irrelevant and embarked upon a degree course at Sheffield University, during which time I did not give much thought to God in any way whatsoever. After leaving university in 1975 I had a few jobs before I joined the West Midlands Police in 1981. During the probationary period, when new recruits had to attend a training day once a month at the Divisional Headquarters, I came into contact with the Christian Police Association (C.P.A.). Their representative was a very plausible person and during his forty minutes presentation I felt pangs of remorse and a sense of guilt. I truly believe that had he produced a commitment card there and then I would have signed it! These convictions were soon to pass and faded into the recesses of my mind. I continued being as dead to God as ever.

So for four years I continued in a worldly existence, not much troubled by convictions of any sort, until July 1985, when it pleased the Lord to cause a severe financial crisis to occur in my household. So severe was it that total ruin was imminent, as every door and avenue of escape was closed to me. This necessitated the selling of some of our possessions to keep us. I confessed that I saw much of God in this matter at the time and inclined myself towards him a little, but I did not seek him diligently or cry unto him for mercy. Therefore as the crisis abated and matters were more in hand, the convictions that flooded in soon passed.

Then in November that year I was struck down with an illness called Sarcoidosis, I was confined to my bed for a while. It was during this period that I began to read the Book of the Revelation. I had begun to read this book because some Russelites—'Jehovah's Witnesses', falsely so-called—had been calling regularly, engaging my wife, Barbara, and myself in arguments about religious matters. Due to my Roman Catholic upbringing I contended with them over the deity of the Lord Jesus Christ and the Holy Spirit. They were studying the Book of the Revelation at the time and I was moved to read it to show them their error. This is what I foolishly imagined, for I had little appreciation at this time of how God was to take a hand in matters and so utterly change my life for ever.

Whilst reading this blessed scripture there came upon me deep impressions of the second death and the lake of fire, the great and notable day of the Lord. I longed to be saved from this and have my sins forgiven. I experienced a dramatic change within me, I was convicted that God was dealing with me in a signal way at this time. I professed to be 'born again' and praised the Lord for such mercy. Assuming then that this was the end of the matter and all was secured finally between God and myself, I was allowed to sojourn in this comfortable delusion and vain presumption for a little season. Oh what a great God we have, He is mighty to save!

I became involved with an evangelical Anglican mission 'church', who were very friendly—cooing and fussing over me —what they didn't do to make me feel welcome! A new convert to boost their numbers, and a policeman to boot! Through their influence I read a vast amount of Billy Graham's works, (all of these have long since been eradicated from my home) but this was all a light healing and daubing with untempered mortar, so much chaff! I attended a men's bible study, only to find it usually degenerated into worldly conversation. This disquieted me for I felt I was very zealous for the Lord and much of what I saw was loose and frivolous. At this time I was experiencing much of the quickening influences of the Holy Spirit, temptations were pouring in upon me like a flood, slips and falls were experienced and I began to be downcast and despair. When I sought comfort from others about these experiences I was told I was 'leaking the Spirit', whatever that meant, how base and rotten it all was. Still I continued with them, not yet deeply convicted to separate from them.

In October 1986 I returned to work, better but not quite fully recovered. Now I began to read 'The Pilgrim's Progress', Mr. Bunyan, how I do thank the Lord for this dear man's works, what comfort he has given me. For the first time I had really deep convictions of sin, sinfulness, utter depravity and my vileness before the Lord. These flooded into my soul and

I was ready to faint with it all. I trembled greatly at the description of the valley of the shadow of death. My distress was total and no man could comfort me, neither would I let them. This was truly the work of God and what God brought me into only God would lead me out of. I had no idea what a wilderness it would be, a barren waste howling wilderness, or what length of time I would be in it; had I known what the Lord was to do with me, I believe I would have feared and trembled even more than I did then. As he dealt with me inwardly the Spirit of God showed me outwardly what rottenness and corruption abounded in Christendom. I praise the Lord for his great mercy shown unto me that he did not allow me to dally in these broken cisterns for overlong.

A short while after my return to work I became a member of the Christian Police Association and was invited to go with them to various places to bear 'witness' as to what God was doing in the Police Force. Here I came into contact with charismatic 'worship' for the first time; my spirit groaned within me. How the Lord has preserved me from the hands of wicked men! The man who conducted the seminar all those years ago at the beginning of my Police service was now the Secretary of the C.P.A. branch. On one occasion he flaunted the 'gifts' of prophecy, tongues, healing, preaching, interpretation and deliverance, I do believe he claimed apostleship also. His preaching was truly amazing, as he suddenly acquired an American accent! Although I was not very pleased about the charismatic element, I still went along and when the time came I duly stood up and gave a 'testimony' of how Jesus saved me. For this I am thoroughly ashamed and have asked forgiveness of my God for such foolish and vain jangling on my part.

I became disillusioned with the Anglicans and sought something more godly, desiring to be fed as I wasted away for need of spiritual food and drink. Yea, I truly began to hunger and thirst. I went to an American fundamentalist evangelical mission called Calvary Chapel. Here I heard fiery preaching which I presumed, though wrongly as I was to discover, was from the glory, this surely was the word of God? I was again courted, it seemed that a Christian Policeman was quite a novelty. When I began to pour out my heart to these people I did not get very much comfort. In fact I cannot remember very much advice, exhorting, building up or comfort whatsoever. I do remember sickly smiles and what I now know was feigned love. They railed on all other denominations but never built up where they tore down. They never fed me, for I was so hungry and thirsty and desired the true word of God more than anything else.

Still the lessons from 'The Pilgrim's Progress' remained with me. I comforted myself with the word of God in the bible and I began to realise that total separation from worldly denominations was the only answer. This, of a truth, met with much opposition and whilst I still attended Calvary Chapel and the bible study I was increasingly perplexed and astonished at the lack of real godliness and sincerity amongst these people who claimed to be the 'elect'.

As the Lord dealt with me inwardly I had much affliction, and temptations continually beset me. These physicians of no value and miserable comforters could offer me nothing for my bruised and battered soul, but I knew that there was balm in Gilead, yea and a Physician there also. I continually sought God's will in these matters and witnessed to these Christian 'brethren' of what I had learnt of God, but to no avail; it seemed quite dark and hopeless.

That is until the day the Lord caused me to come across a copy of 'The Messiah' in a local bookshop. Oh blessed day! I read it avidly, here was food indeed. This spoke of my pilgrimage, of mourning, of hungering and thirsting. It was an answer to prayer, and how the Lord prospered me to obtain a copy still fills me with excitement now as I can recall my reading some of the pages just after I had purchased it. Oh how joy sprang up within me for such a treasure as this. I set about reading all of Mr. Metcalfe's works as I could find in the different bookshops. I tried to share my joy but was met with little interest and much indifference.

About this time I made contact with the Publishing Trust and also my beloved brother John Darroch. John Darroch encouraged me and helped me with many of my burdens. From the first time I spoke to him on the telephone I knew I had a token of what was real and true, for my spirit was at one with this man, I felt I had always known him so comfortable was the conversation with him. John advised me to keep in touch and to begin having the tape ministry of the Lord's servant.

When I heard Mr. Metcalfe preach, how it affected me—here was the word of the Lord from the glory—how it caused me to have tremendous and deeply searching convictions of my utter depravity, sinfulness and vile, corrupt nature. How I especially cleaved to the preaching of Psalm 11 and Romans 3:28. I tried to get others interested in this ministry but met with much deadness. John Darroch was a continual source of comfort and my one link with real religion, for I was now really convicted very deeply of the futility, even sinfulness, of remaining in any of the denominations. I had read 'The Red Heifer' and feared and trembled at the stern warnings contained therein.

In November 1987 the Lord, in his merciful bounty and lovingkindness blessed us with a son, Luke. This was truly an answer to prayer. I gave thanks to God for such a gift and I prayed then, as I do now, that I would bring him up in the fear and admonition of the Lord. At this time I began to be outspoken amongst the Christian 'brethren' with regard to what had been revealed to me of the Lord Jesus Christ concerning his body, the true church, and how one must be separated, pure, with a clear division from all that is of man, cleaving only to what is of God. Invariably I met with opposition in whatever I said regarding these matters, but for all their rebukes, reviling and coldness it was the footsteps of the flock I was following, the valley of Baca I sojourned in, and God had put me there, so no man was going to dissuade me in any way. It was the strait gate and the narrow way that I loved, and desired no other way.

In February 1988 I was struck down again with my illness, and though it was a bitter blow I knew it was of the Lord and all things would work for the good. At this time I met with much adversity from the professing 'churches' because I spoke of separation and being 'outside the camp'. But I wouldn't compromise and I was rebuked and the finger wagged at me; even though I was very, very poorly all this was heaped upon me by these 'Christians'. It was a sore trial but I bore it for the Lord Jesus and his truth, for he had borne much, much more for me. Even though I suffered physically through it I lay nothing to their charge and forgive them for their hardness and insensitivity. For by him I had been led into this and no man would lead me out, never!

I could truly say that the Lord's dealings with me at this time were such that the furnace of affliction and I were good companions for nigh on the rest of the year and this coupled with a perverse and crooked people afflicting me at various times I could own the scripture, 'They wandered in the wilderness in a solitary way; they found no city to dwell in. Hungry and thirsty, their soul fainted in them. Then they cried unto the LORD in their trouble, and he delivered them out of their distresses. And he led them forth by the right way, that they might go to a city of habitation.' Yet will I praise the Lord for his tender mercies and lovingkindness towards me, for though he did not spare the rod, he gave me many tokens of his love.

I eventually managed to visit the brethren at Tylers Green. It was for a first day meeting and John Darroch was to collect me from Euston Station. I saw him before he saw me and I knew it was him, what joy, for here was a man I had never seen but I knew he was my brother in Christ. For the Spirit within me ratified the bond that exists between those that are of the body of our Lord Jesus Christ, it is unmistakable and inimitable; I have never felt anything like it before. At the meeting—what fervent prayer, what fear was upon the assembly—this was what the Lord had preserved me for all this time. I was home among my brethren. Here was godliness, here was a sober people. Oh how I gave thanks, how I praised the Lord. I could not contain my joy. I will never forget that day.

I was pensioned out of the Police Force due to ill health in February 1989. I saw this was of God and gave thanks, 'It is the LORD, let him do what seemeth him good.' I was much blessed at this time by tokens and manifestations of the Lord Jesus Christ's love towards me. I profited from the writings of Mr. Metcalfe and past servants of the Lord. I was built up and edified from hearing Mr. Metcalfe preach both on tape and in the assembly. On this occasion I was most uplifted and scarcely able to say anything to the Lord's servant, much less see him, for the tears of joy and the fear that was inside me from hearing such powerful preaching. The Lord be praised for his faithful labourer in the vineyard!

But despite all this that was bestowed upon me I let much slip and the Lord was not slow in chastening me for this. I had not fixed my eye on the Lord Jesus and consequently was found languishing in sorrow and despair. I cried unto the Lord that he would incline his ear unto me, that he would not rebuke me in his hot displeasure. I sought smiles not frowns. I cried night and day unto the Lord to deliver me. I was never so downcast.

But the Lord heard my cry, he inclined his ear unto me. My faith was strengthened and I was blessed with such powerful manifestations of the love of the Lord Jesus Christ that I could barely stand. The love and mercy that has been shown me by my Lord has in many ways been revealed to me, even up to this moment and I give thanks and praise, marvelling at the 'love of Christ which passeth knowledge'. I covet every precious moment of this blessed 'time of refreshing' for I realise that of a certainty there shall be fresh trials, temptations and afflictions to come.

So I have in a brief way given a testimony as to the dealings of the Lord with me these past four years, it seems longer than that and much has happened in that time, but whereas I was ashamed of what I called a testimony before, I am not ashamed of this; for what has happened to me has been all of God and none of man, I look to him and him alone for salvation, of myself I can do nothing, therefore as I know it was God that called me by grace and revealed his Son in me I can now say 'I believed, therefore I spake'.

As a consequence of this I seek to be baptised, giving thanks unto God that he has kept me from the hands of unclean men until this time and if it is his will I pray that his servant will be enabled to fulfil my earnest desire. I give thanks to my Lord and Master that I have been enabled by his Spirit to accomplish this, my testimony.

And now I give thanks unto God the Father for his Son who is the shepherd of my soul and whose voice I have heard calling me these past years. Which voice I have sought to follow wholeheartedly as I was enabled, and when I erred and strayed, many times, how he came and found me, set me on his shoulders to bring me, with much rejoicing, back to the fold. How he has found me in the way, bruised and cut through many trials and afflictions, then nestling my head in his bosom he has washed my wounds and poured in oil and wine, binding them up.

Oh, when I was disobedient he did send the north winds to beat at my back and drive me to him and when I mourned sore like a dove, he drew me to him with south winds bringing sweet odours from his garden, and I was drawn to him by his lovingkindness, a love that was from everlasting. Yea for all this to me he is worth thousands of gold. He is the chiefest among ten thousand and altogether lovely.

I do bless his holy name and give thanks and praise always in his name: Our Lord Jesus Christ. Amen and Amen.

Paul Giles

The Conversion of Sean Cook

Derby

13th April, 1990

Dear Mr. Metcalfe,

I was brought up in a village near Derby, but I was not brought up in a religious way. Apart from going once or twice to the Methodist Sunday School I had never anything to do with religion.

When I left school, instead of going into my father's firm as everyone expected, I joined the army. I was looking for independence and adventure, and, because I had already been in the army cadets from the age of fourteen, I believed the army would give me what I wanted.

After one year's training at Folkstone, where everything seemed to go smoothly, I was sent to Germany for six months with my battalion, 'The Worcester and Sherwood Foresters'. However in Germany things soon began to go wrong. This was mostly due to keeping company with many of the older men and taking on their bad ways.

My next posting, after spending a year at Warminster (England), was to Northern Ireland, where I was based at Aldergrove for five months. During this time we patrolled the border around Fermanagh with the R.U.C.

Coming back to England from Ulster, I found life very dull, so I took a fortnight's leave. But, between one thing and another, I was three days late in returning to camp at the end of my leave. I knew that if I went back now I would be jailed for being absent, so, on impulse, I took a flight out to Tenerife, where I spent the time working in bars and taking on casual work. But when work dried up, and I got short of money, along with two others I burgled a shop. On what I made out of this I managed to get to Majorca where my parents have a house. There I stayed for two months.

At first I asked God to get me out of all this trouble. For days I really did think that God was punishing me for what I had done. I promised him that if I got out of the mess I was in I would change and reform. But as things got a little easier all my promises were forgotten.

I flew back to the U.K. around the end of that year, and after ten days, handed myself in to the army. But because I had come back of my own accord to sort things out, they let me return to my company until the court martial came up.

After the court martial I was sent to the Corrective Training Centre at Colchester for three months. I got a third remission for good behaviour and rejoined my unit which was going to Cyprus.

One night in Cyprus I again broke the rules, taking an army Land Rover so that me and my mates could go on a spree. The place we went to was in a forbidden area: no army vehicle should have been there. For this breach I was jailed for three weeks.

While I was in the cell in the unit guardroom I found a bible and some tracts which I spent a considerable time reading. I found out from the tracts that I could get right with God by saying a prayer and committing my life to the Lord. I said the prayer: nothing happened. So I said it again, and must have said it several times before I was visited by the man from the 'Soldiers' and Airmen's Scripture Readers Association' (SASRA) who had himself placed the bible and tracts. I told him that I had read a certain tract and said the prayer at the back. When he heard this he assured me that I was converted and started me on some 'Emmaus' bible courses which told me how I should behave now that I was 'converted' and all about conversion not being a matter of feelings but something which was just to be 'believed'.

When I came out of jail I began to attend the 'Christian Fellowship'. This involved going to bible studies and prayer meetings. I did this for about three months. Then it was back to the U.K. and the termination of my three year contract.

Once I was home I started attending the Baptist church in the next village. The people seemed to be interested in me and they appeared delighted with my testimony. I told my parents that I was now 'attending church' and they came along to support me. They liked it themselves and settled in. My fiancée also began to come to the meetings.

It was not long before I felt that there was something missing in my life. When I had been in Cyprus I had heard Charismatics speaking about the 'baptism of the Holy Spirit'; I wondered if this was what I lacked. At the same time I did not want what they claimed to have. Some time later, after I had read your tract 'The Charismatic Delusion', it was confirmed to me that they did not have what I wanted.

Another thing that troubled me while I was attending the Baptist church was that you could not get anyone to the prayer-meeting. They did not mind the 'Men's Meeting', you could get thirty at that for singing practice.

Meanwhile I was going round giving my testimony. I became quite well known in certain evangelical circles. One man who heard me invited me to give my testimony at his meeting. Up until now I had not read many of your tracts. But once I had, a few months later, especially 'Faith or Presumption?' I began to be really exercised as to whether or not I should go to this man's meeting.

However, after a while I thought it might be a good chance to tell people what I was experiencing. So I went and told them and it went down like a rock. Nearly everybody there had already heard my testimony, and had come to hear it again. I told them that I didn't really feel that I was converted, and if there was anyone else who felt like this they should make sure that they got their assurance from God. Afterwards one woman said to me, 'We were not expecting you to say that, we have brought our friends to hear your testimony and you have told us something different.' But I could have told them nothing else. The Lord had taken away my vain confidence and false assurance.

Now my friends, seeing the change in me, began to warn me against reading your tracts. The Baptist church leader was one of these. I had loaned him a copy of 'Noah and the Flood'. Afterwards he raged against it and said that what you had written was not in the scriptures. But the next first-day, when he was preaching, he told us that the blood of Christ was first of all before God, and then before man, which I knew was exactly what he got through reading your book and putting it in his sermon!

At last I felt that I had to come down to Tylers Green and speak to someone. I arrived one Saturday in January last year, spent the night in the car, and came to the meeting next morning. Afterwards John Nichol asked me back to his house for lunch. I came down to the meetings a few more times and then decided that I would not be going back to the Baptist church. 'How can two walk together except they be agreed?'

On one of my visits to Tylers Green, while I was sitting waiting for the afternoon prayer meeting to begin, I began to be really concerned about my parents. I was really cut up that they were completely hardened against the truth, the ministry, and the brethren. But as I was sitting the Lord said to me, 'Behold thy mother and thy brethren.' I realised who were my real parents, and who were my real brethren, and that was a great comfort to me.

The time of my deliverance came recently while I was at home listening to a tape of your preaching on Psalm 114. It was the last verse. There had been times when I was rebuked through reading the testimonies of other brethren. There had been with me almost an unwillingness to credit the work of God. Now as I listened to the tape I realised what the Lord had done in turning the rock into a standing water. It was not something I was to look for in the future. I was to look back and see that the work had already been done in Christ, upon the cross, on my behalf. That was when I had the real assurance that I was saved.

Yours most sincerely,

Sean Cook

Derby
18th April, 1990

Dear Mr. Metcalfe,

I do thank the God and Father of our Lord Jesus Christ for that which thou didst deliver unto us this first day evening past. What love and joy and peace is brought to the heart when Jesus Christ is set forth evidently crucified among us.

Oh how gracious is our God and Father that we should be given such a sight of his Son and be brought to such a place as this from whence to view it. For I know that in me, that is, in my flesh, dwelleth no good thing. Therefore how good it is to have the eyes drawn from oneself to look upon him who loved us and gave himself for us.

What a different state of heart and spirit this brings in. What glory, what love, what heavenliness is seen in the Son which dwelleth in the bosom of the Father and would that we should dwell in him. How good it is to see the Sun of righteousness in the heavens, to feel the healing from his wings, to hear his voice and follow him into the heavens, to be enabled to walk in the light that streams from the glory, and to have the cold within replaced by warmth and light: 'Thy word is to my feet a lamp and to my path a light.'

Now the winter is passed, the cold is replaced by the warmth of the love of Christ. The darkness giveth place to the light which cometh from the glory. The dead numbness of unbelief giveth place to faith and newness of life. 'If any man be in Christ, he is a new creature: old things are passed away; behold, all things are become new. And all things are of God, who hath reconciled us to himself by Jesus Christ.'

Surely it is a good thing to give thanks unto our God and sing praises unto his holy name.

The Almighty God be with thee to strengthen and bless thee for his dear name's sake.

Sean Cook

To: Sean Cook High Wycombe,
From: John Metcalfe Bucks.

23rd April, 1990

My Dear Brother,

Grace be unto thee, mercy and peace, from God our Father, and the Lord Jesus Christ, the Son of the Father, in truth and love.

Your letter brought great consolation in Christ, and comfort of the Holy Ghost, and I am assured that this is the faith of God's elect. To see Christ crucified, to value his precious blood, this is to bring to saving faith. But to voice what you have now expressed with joy, to sound out your rejoicing in the Son of God in the glory, to triumph in him, to glory in the Man in the presence of God and the Father on our behalf, in light unapproachable, in whom we have acceptance, by whose blood we are justified: this is the full assurance of faith, and the very witness of the Holy Ghost from heaven.

To hear you so speak of Christ: so edifying, so comforting. For months and months past this has been my constant prayer for you. When one has so laboured in prayer, to hear from the very person for whom one has thus travailed, and to hear the same words as those so long carried before the throne of grace in intercession on his behalf: who can express the joy this brings?

Go on in this thy strength, thou mighty man of valour, go on—through darkness, hardship, cruel mockings, persecutions, afflictions: go on—to the very end, and the God of all grace be with thee. Thy providences, and those of thy faithful wife, are ever before me. Nothing but his will: not ours; not man's. The grace of our Lord Jesus Christ be with you both in all your pathway to glory.

Now the God of hope fill you with all joy and peace in believing, that ye may abound in hope, through the power of the Holy Ghost.

My love in Christ
to my dear brother and sister,

John Metcalfe

Now when they saw the boldness of Peter and John, and perceived that they were unlearned and ignorant men, they marvelled; and they took knowledge of them, that they had been with Jesus.
And beholding the man which was healed standing with them, THEY COULD SAY NOTHING AGAINST IT.

Acts of the Apostles Chapter 4 verses 13,14.

THE END

INDEX

TO OTHER PUBLICATIONS

PSALMS, HYMNS AND SPIRITUAL SONGS

iv

THE PSALMS

OF THE

OLD TESTAMENT

The Psalms of the Old Testament, the result of years of painstaking labour, is an original translation into verse from the Authorised Version, which seeks to present the Psalms in the purest scriptural form possible for singing. Here, for the first time, divine names are rendered as and when they occur in the scripture, the distinction between Lord and Lord has been preserved, and every essential point of doctrine and experience appears with unique perception and fidelity.

The Psalms of the Old Testament is the first part of a trilogy written by John Metcalfe, the second part of which is entitled *Spiritual Songs from the Gospels*, and the last, *The Hymns of the New Testament*. These titles provide unique and accurate metrical versions of passages from the psalms, the gospels and the new testament epistles respectively, and are intended to be used together in the worship of God.

Price £2.50 *(postage extra)*
(hard-case binding, dust-jacket)
ISBN 0 9506366 7 3

SPIRITUAL SONGS

FROM

THE GOSPELS

The *Spiritual Songs from the Gospels*, the result of years of painstaking labour, is an original translation into verse from the Authorised Version, which seeks to present essential parts of the gospels in the purest scriptural form possible for singing. The careful selection from Matthew, Mark, Luke and John, set forth in metrical verse of the highest integrity, enables the singer to sing 'the word of Christ' as if from the scripture itself, 'richly and in all wisdom'; and, above all, in a way that facilitates worship in song of unprecedented fidelity.

The *Spiritual Songs from the Gospels* is the central part of a trilogy written by John Metcalfe, the first part of which is entitled *The Psalms of the Old Testament*, and the last, *The Hymns of the New Testament*. These titles provide unique and accurate metrical versions of passages from the psalms, the gospels and the new testament epistles respectively, and are intended to be used together in the worship of God.

Price £2.50 *(postage extra)*
(hard-case binding, dust-jacket)
ISBN 0 9506366 8 1

THE HYMNS

OF THE

NEW TESTAMENT

The *Hymns of the New Testament*, the result of years of painstaking labour, is an original translation into verse from the Authorised Version, which presents essential parts of the new testament epistles in the purest scriptural form possible for singing. The careful selection from the book of Acts to that of Revelation, set forth in metrical verse of the highest integrity, enables the singer to sing 'the word of Christ' as if from the scripture itself, 'richly and in all wisdom'; and, above all, in a way that facilitates worship in song of unprecedented fidelity.

The *Hymns of the New Testament* is the last part of a trilogy written by John Metcalfe, the first part of which is entitled *The Psalms of the Old Testament*, and the next, *Spiritual Songs from the Gospels*. These titles provide unique and accurate metrical versions of passages from the psalms, the gospels and the new testament epistles respectively, and are intended to be used together in the worship of God.

Price £2.50 *(postage extra)*
(hard-case binding, dust-jacket)
ISBN 0 9506366 9 X

'THE APOSTOLIC FOUNDATION
OF THE
CHRISTIAN CHURCH' SERIES

FOUNDATIONS UNCOVERED

THE APOSTOLIC FOUNDATION
OF THE
CHRISTIAN CHURCH

Volume I

Foundations Uncovered is a small book of some 37 pages. This is the introduction to the major series: 'The Apostolic Foundation of the Christian Church'.

Rich in truth, the Introduction deals comprehensively with the foundation of the apostolic faith under the descriptive titles: The Word, The Doctrine, The Truth, The Gospel, The Faith, The New Testament, and The Foundation.

The contents of the book reveal: The Fact of the Foundation; The Foundation Uncovered; What the Foundation is not; How the Foundation is Described; and, Being Built upon the Foundation.

'This book comes with the freshness of a new Reformation.'

Price 30p *(postage extra)*
(Laminated cover)
ISBN 0 9506366 5 7

THE BIRTH OF JESUS CHRIST

THE APOSTOLIC FOUNDATION
OF THE
CHRISTIAN CHURCH

Volume II

'The very spirit of adoration and worship rings through the pages of *The Birth of Jesus Christ*.

'The author expresses with great clarity the truths revealed to him in his study of holy scriptures at depth. We are presented here with a totally lofty view of the Incarnation.

'John Metcalfe is to be classed amongst the foremost expositors of our age; and his writings have about them that quality of timelessness that makes me sure they will one day take their place among the heritage of truly great Christian works.'

From a review by Rev. David Catterson.

'Uncompromisingly faithful to scripture ... has much to offer which is worth serious consideration ... deeply moving.'

The Expository Times.

Price 95p *(postage extra)*
(Laminated Cover)
ISBN 0 9502515 5 0

THE MESSIAH

THE APOSTOLIC FOUNDATION
OF THE
CHRISTIAN CHURCH

Volume III

The Messiah is a spiritually penetrating and entirely original exposition of Matthew chapter one to chapter seven from the trenchant pen of John Metcalfe.

Matthew Chapters One to Seven

GENEALOGY · BIRTH · STAR OF BETHLEHEM
HEROD · FLIGHT TO EGYPT · NAZARETH
JOHN THE BAPTIST · THE BAPTIST'S MINISTRY
JESUS' BAPTISM · ALL RIGHTEOUSNESS FULFILLED
HEAVEN OPENED · THE SPIRIT'S DESCENT
THE TEMPTATION OF JESUS IN THE WILDERNESS
JESUS' MANIFESTATION · THE CALLING · THE TRUE DISCIPLES
THE BEATITUDES · THE SERMON ON THE MOUNT

'Something of the fire of the ancient Hebrew prophet .... Metcalfe has spiritual and expository potentials of a high order.'

The Life of Faith.

Price £2.45 *(postage extra)*
(425 pages, Laminated Cover)
ISBN 0 9502515 8 5

THE SON OF GOD AND SEED OF DAVID

THE APOSTOLIC FOUNDATION
OF THE
CHRISTIAN CHURCH

Volume IV

The Son of God and Seed of David is the fourth volume in the major work entitled 'The Apostolic Foundation of the Christian Church.'

'The author proceeds to open and allege that Jesus Christ is and ever was *The Son of God*. This greatest of subjects, this most profound of all mysteries, is handled with reverence and with outstanding perception.

'The second part considers *The Seed of David*. What is meant precisely by 'the seed'? And why 'of David'? With prophetic insight the author expounds these essential verities.'

Price £6.95 *(postage extra)*
Hardback 250 pages
Laminated bookjacket
ISBN 1 870039 16 5

CHRIST CRUCIFIED

THE APOSTOLIC FOUNDATION
OF THE
CHRISTIAN CHURCH

Volume V

Christ Crucified the definitive work on the crucifixion, the blood, and the cross of Jesus Christ.

The crucifixion of Jesus Christ witnessed in the Gospels: the gospel according to Matthew; Mark; Luke; John.

The blood of Jesus Christ declared in the Epistles: the shed blood; the blood of purchase; redemption through his blood; the blood of sprinkling; the blood of the covenant.

The doctrine of the cross revealed in the apostolic foundation of the Christian church: the doctrine of the cross; the cross and the body of sin; the cross and the carnal mind; the cross and the law; the offence of the cross; the cross of our Lord Jesus Christ.

Price £6.95 *(postage extra)*
Hardback 300 pages
Laminated bookjacket
ISBN 1 870039 08 4

JUSTIFICATION BY FAITH

THE APOSTOLIC FOUNDATION
OF THE
CHRISTIAN CHURCH

Volume VI

THE HEART OF THE GOSPEL · THE FOUNDATION OF THE CHURCH
THE ISSUE OF ETERNITY
CLEARLY, ORIGINALLY AND POWERFULLY OPENED

The basis · The righteousness of the law
The righteousness of God · The atonement · Justification
Traditional views considered · Righteousness imputed to faith
Faith counted for righteousness · Justification by Faith

'And it came to pass, when Jesus had ended these sayings, the people were astonished at his doctrine: for he taught them as one having authority, and not as the scribes.' Matthew 7:28,29.

Price £7.50 *(postage extra)*
Hardback 375 pages
Laminated bookjacket
ISBN 1870039 11 4

THE CHURCH: WHAT IS IT?

THE APOSTOLIC FOUNDATION
OF THE
CHRISTIAN CHURCH

Volume VII

The answer to this question proceeds first from the lips of Jesus himself, Mt. 16:18, later to be expounded by the words of the apostles whom he sent.

Neither fear of man nor favour from the world remotely affect the answer.

Here is the truth, the whole truth, and nothing but the truth.

The complete originality, the vast range, and the total fearlessness of this book command the attention in a way that is unique.

Read this book: you will never read another like it.

Outspokenly devastating yet devastatingly constructive.

Price £7.75 (postage extra)
Hardback 400 pages
Laminated bookjacket
ISBN 1 870039 23 8

OTHER TITLES

NOAH AND THE FLOOD

Noah and the Flood expounds with vital urgency the man and the message that heralded the end of the old world. The description of the flood itself is vividly realistic. The whole work has an unmistakable ring of authority, and speaks as 'Thus saith the Lord'.

'Mr. Metcalfe makes a skilful use of persuasive eloquence as he challenges the reality of one's profession of faith ... he gives a rousing call to a searching self-examination and evaluation of one's spiritual experience.'

The Monthly Record of the Free Church of Scotland.

Price £1.90 *(postage extra)*
(Laminated Cover)
ISBN 1 870039 22 X

DIVINE FOOTSTEPS

Divine Footsteps traces the pathway of the feet of the Son of man from the very beginning in the prophetic figures of the true in the old testament through the reality in the new; doing so in a way of experimental spirituality. At the last a glimpse of the coming glory is beheld as his feet are viewed as standing at the latter day upon the earth.

Price 95p *(postage extra)*
(Laminated Cover)
ISBN 1 870039 21 1

THE RED HEIFER

The Red Heifer was the name given to a sacrifice used by the children of Israel in the Old Testament—as recorded in Numbers 19—in which a heifer was slain and burned. Cedar wood, hyssop and scarlet were cast into the burning, and the ashes were mingled with running water and put in a vessel. It was kept for the children of Israel for a water of separation: it was a purification for sin.

In this unusual book the sacrifice is brought up to date and its relevance to the church today is shown.

Price 75p *(postage extra)*
ISBN 0 9502515 4 2

THE WELLS OF SALVATION

The Wells of Salvation is written from a series of seven powerful addresses preached at Tylers Green. It is a forthright and experimental exposition of Isaiah 12:3, 'Therefore with joy shall ye draw water out of the wells of salvation.'

Price £1.50 *(postage extra)*
(Laminated Cover)
ISBN 0 9502515 6 9

OF GOD OR MAN?

LIGHT FROM GALATIANS

The Epistle to the Galatians contends for deliverance from the law and from carnal ministry.

The Apostle opens his matter in two ways:

Firstly, Paul vindicates himself and his ministry against those that came not from God above, but from Jerusalem below.

Secondly, he defends the Gospel and evangelical liberty against legal perversions and bondage to the flesh.

Price £1.45 *(postage extra)*
(Laminated Cover)
ISBN 0 9506366 3 0

A QUESTION FOR POPE JOHN PAUL II

As a consequence of his many years spent apart in prayer, lonely vigil, and painstaking study of the scripture, John Metcalfe asks a question and looks for an answer from Pope John Paul II.

Price £1.25. *(postage extra)*
(Laminated Cover)
ISBN 0 9506366 4 9

THE BOOK OF RUTH

The Book of Ruth is set against the farming background of old testament Israel at the time of the Judges, the narrative—unfolding the work of God in redemption—being marked by a series of agricultural events.

These events—the famine; the barley harvest; the wheat harvest; the winnowing—possessed a hidden spiritual significance to that community, but, much more, they speak in figure directly to our own times, as the book reveals.

Equally contemporary appear the characters of Ruth, Naomi, Boaz, and the first kinsman, drawn with spiritual perception greatly to the profit of the reader.

Price £4.95 *(postage extra)*
Hardback 200 pages
Laminated bookjacket
ISBN 1 870039 17 3

NEWLY PUBLISHED

The Trust announces the publication
of two new titles

PRESENT-DAY CONVERSIONS
OF THE NEW TESTAMENT KIND

FROM THE MINISTRY OF

JOHN METCALFE

Price £2.25 *(postage extra)*
(Laminated Cover)
ISBN 1 870039 31 9

DIVINE MEDITATIONS

OF

WILLIAM HUNTINGTON

Price £2.35 *(postage extra)*
(Laminated Cover)
ISBN 1 870039 24 6

'TRACT FOR THE TIMES' SERIES

THE GOSPEL OF GOD

'TRACT FOR THE TIMES' SERIES

The Gospel of God. Beautifully designed, this tract positively describes the gospel under the following headings: The Gospel is of God; The Gospel is Entirely of God; The Gospel is Entire in Itself; The Gospel is Preached; The Gospel Imparts Christ; and, Nothing But the Gospel Imparts Christ.

Price 25p *(postage extra)*
(Laminated Cover)
No. 1 in the Series

THE STRAIT GATE

'TRACT FOR THE TIMES' SERIES

The Strait Gate. Exceptionally well made, this booklet consists of extracts from 'The Messiah', compiled in such a way as to challenge the shallowness of much of today's 'easy-believism', whilst positively pointing to the strait gate.

Price 25p *(postage extra)*
(Laminated Cover)
No. 2 in the Series

ETERNAL SONSHIP
AND TAYLOR BRETHREN

'TRACT FOR THE TIMES' SERIES

Eternal Sonship and Taylor Brethren. This booklet is highly recommended, particularly for those perplexed by James Taylor's teaching against the eternal sonship of Christ.

Price 25p *(postage extra)*
(Laminated Cover)
No. 3 in the Series

MARKS OF THE
NEW TESTAMENT CHURCH
'TRACT FOR THE TIMES' SERIES

Marks of the New Testament Church. This exposition from Acts 2:42 declares what were, and what were not, the abiding marks of the church. The apostles' doctrine, fellowship and ordinances are lucidly explained.

Price 25p *(postage extra)*
(Laminated Cover)
No. 4 in the Series

THE CHARISMATIC DELUSION
'TRACT FOR THE TIMES' SERIES

The Charismatic Delusion. A prophetic message revealing the fundamental error of this movement which has swept away so many in the tide of its popularity. Here the delusion is dispelled.

Price 25p *(postage extra)*
(Laminated Cover)
No. 5 in the Series

PREMILLENNIALISM EXPOSED
'TRACT FOR THE TIMES' SERIES

Premillennialism Exposed. Well received evangelically, particularly through the influence of J.N. Darby, the Schofield bible, and the Plymouth Brethren, Premillennialism has assumed the cloak of orthodoxy. In this tract the cloak is removed, and the unorthodoxy of this system is exposed. A remarkable revelation.

Price 25p *(postage extra)*
(Laminated Cover)
No. 6 in the Series

JUSTIFICATION AND PEACE

'TRACT FOR THE TIMES' SERIES

Justification and Peace. This tract is taken from a message preached in December 1984 at Penang Hill, Malaysia. In this well-known address, peace with God is seen to be based upon nothing save justification by faith. No one should miss this tract.

Price 25p *(postage extra)*
(Laminated Cover)
No. 7 in the Series

FAITH OR PRESUMPTION?

'TRACT FOR THE TIMES' SERIES

Faith or presumption? The eighth tract in this vital series exposes the difference between faith and presumption, showing that faith is not of the law, neither is is apart from the work of God, nor is it of man. The work of God in man that precedes saving faith is opened generally and particularly, and the tract goes on to reveal positively the nature of saving faith. Belief and 'easy-believism' are contrasted, making clear the difference between the two, as the system of presumption—called easy-believism—is clearly shown, and the way of true belief pointed out with lucid clarity.

Price 25p *(postage extra)*
(Laminated Cover)
No. 8 in the Series

THE ELECT UNDECEIVED

'TRACT FOR THE TIMES' SERIES

The Elect undeceived, the ninth Tract for the Times, earnestly contends for 'the faith once delivered to the saints' in a way that is spiritually edifying, positive, and subject to the Lord Jesus Christ according to the scriptures.

The Tract is a response to the pamphlet 'Salvation and the Church' published jointly by the Catholic Truth Society and Church House Publishing, in which the Anglican and Roman Catholic Commissioners agree together about JUSTIFICATION. The pamphlet shows how they have agreed.

Price 25p *(postage extra)*
(Laminated Cover)
No. 9 in the Series

JUSTIFYING RIGHTEOUSNESS

'TRACT FOR THE TIMES' SERIES

Justifying Righteousness. Was it wrought by the law of Moses or by the blood of Christ? Written not in the language of dead theology but that of the living God, here is the vital and experimental doctrine of the new testament. Part of the book 'Justification by Faith', nevertheless this tract has a message in itself essential to those who would know and understand the truth.

Price 25p *(postage extra)*
(Laminated Cover)
No. 10 in the Series

RIGHTEOUSNESS IMPUTED

'TRACT FOR THE TIMES' SERIES

Righteousness Imputed. The truth of the gospel and the fallacy of tradition. Here the gospel trumpet of the jubilee is sounded in no uncertain terms, as on the one hand that truth essential to be believed for salvation is opened from holy scripture, and on the other the errors of Brethrenism are brought to light in a unique and enlightening way. This tract is taken from the book 'Justification by Faith', but in itself it conveys a message of great penetration and clarity.

Price 25p *(postage extra)*
(Laminated Cover)
No. 11 in the Series

THE GREAT DECEPTION

'TRACT FOR THE TIMES' SERIES

The Great Deception. The erosion of Justification by faith. All ministers, every Christian, and each assembly ought not only to possess but to read and reread this prophetic message as the word of the Lord to this generation, set in the context of the age. This tract is part of the book 'Justification by Faith' but contains within itself a message which is at once vital and authoritative.

Price 25p *(postage extra)*
(Laminated Cover)
No. 12 in the Series

A FAMINE IN THE LAND

'TRACT FOR THE TIMES' SERIES

A Famine in the Land. Taken from the Book of Ruth, with telling forcefulness this tract opens conditions exactly parallel to those of our own times. 'Behold, the days come, saith the Lord GOD, that I will send a famine in the land, not a famine of bread, nor a thirst for water, but of hearing the words of the LORD: and they shall wander from sea to sea, and from the north even to the east, they shall run to and fro to seek the word of the LORD, and shall not find it.'

Price 25p *(postage extra)*
(Laminated Cover)
No. 13 in the Series

BLOOD AND WATER

'TRACT FOR THE TIMES' SERIES

Blood and Water. Of the four gospels, only John reveals the truth that blood was shed at the cross. When it was shed, Jesus was dead already. With the blood there came forth water. But what do these things mean? With devastating present-day application, this tract tells you what they mean.

Price 25p *(postage extra)*
(Laminated Cover)
No. 14 in the Series

WOMEN BISHOPS?
'TRACT FOR THE TIMES' SERIES

Women Bishops? This is a question that has arisen in America, but should it have arisen at all?
Read this tract and find out the authoritative answer.

Price 25p *(postage extra)*
(Laminated Cover)
No. 15 in the Series

THE HEAVENLY VISION
'TRACT FOR THE TIMES' SERIES

The Heavenly Vision not only transformed the prophet himself, it became a savour of life unto life—or death unto death—to all the people.
'*Where there is no vision the people perish*', Proverbs 29:18. This is true. But where is the vision today? And what is the vision today? This tract answers those questions.

Price 25p *(Postage extra)*
(Laminated Cover)
No. 16 in the Series

EVANGELICAL TRACTS

EVANGELICAL TRACTS

1. **The Two Prayers of Elijah**. Green card cover, price 10p.

2. **Wounded for our Transgressions**. Gold card cover, price 10p.

3. **The Blood of Sprinkling**. Red card cover, price 10p.

4. **The Grace of God that brings Salvation**. Blue card cover, price 10p.

5. **The Name of Jesus**. Rose card cover, price 10p.

6. **The Ministry of the New Testament**. Purple card cover, price 10p.

7. **The Death of the Righteous** (*The closing days of J.B. Stoney*) by A.M.S. (his daughter). Ivory card cover, Price 10p.

ECCLESIA TRACTS

ECCLESIA TRACTS
NEWLY PUBLISHED

The Beginning of the Ecclesia by John Metcalfe. No. 1 in the Series, Sand grain cover, Price 10p.

Churches and the Church by J.N. Darby. Edited. No. 2 in the Series, Sand grain cover, Price 10p.

The Ministers of Christ by John Metcalfe. No. 3 in the Series, Sand grain cover, Price 10p.

The Inward Witness by George Fox. Edited. No. 4 in the Series, Sand grain cover, Price 10p.

The Notion of a Clergyman by J.N. Darby. Edited. No. 5 in the Series, Sand grain cover, Price 10p.

The Servant of the Lord by William Huntington. Edited and Abridged. No. 6 in the Series, Sand grain cover, Price 10p.

One Spirit by William Kelly. Edited. No. 7 in the Series, Sand grain cover, Price 10p.

The Funeral of Arminianism by William Huntington. Edited and Abridged. No. 8 in the Series, Sand grain cover, Price 10p.

One Body by William Kelly. Edited. No. 9 in the Series, Sand grain cover, Price 10p.

False Churches and True by John Metcalfe. No. 10 in the Series, Sand grain cover, Price 10p.

Separation from Evil by J.N. Darby. Edited. No. 11 in the Series, Sand grain cover, Price 10p.

The Remnant by J.B. Stoney. Edited. No. 12 in the Series, Sand grain cover, Price 10p.

MINISTRY BY JOHN METCALFE

TAPE MINISTRY BY JOHN METCALFE
FROM ENGLAND AND THE FAR EAST
IS AVAILABLE.

In order to obtain this free recorded ministry, please send your blank cassette (C.90) and the cost of the return postage, including your name and address in block capitals, to the John Metcalfe Publishing Trust, Church Road, Tylers Green, Penn, Bucks, HP10 8LN. Tapelists are available on request.

Owing to the increased demand for the tape ministry, we are unable to supply more than two tapes per order, except in the case of meetings for the hearing of tapes, where a special arrangement can be made.

THE MINISTRY OF THE NEW TESTAMENT

The purpose of this substantial A4 gloss paper magazine is to provide spiritual and experimental ministry with sound doctrine which rightly and prophetically divides the Word of Truth.

Readers of our books will already know the high standards of our publications. They can be confident that these pages will maintain that quality, by giving access to enduring ministry from the past, much of which is derived from sources that are virtually unobtainable today, and publishing a living ministry from the present. Selected articles from the following writers have already been included:

ELI ASHDOWN · ABRAHAM BOOTH · JOHN BUNYAN
JOHN BURGON · JOHN CALVIN · DONALD CARGILL
JOHN CENNICK · J.N. DARBY · GEORGE FOX · JOHN FOXE
WILLIAM GADSBY · WILLIAM HUNTINGTON · WILLIAM KELLY
JOHN KENNEDY · JOHN KERSHAW · HANSERD KNOLLYS
JAMES LEWIS · MARTIN LUTHER · ROBERT MURRAY MCCHEYNE
JOHN METCALFE · ALEXANDER—SANDY—PEDEN
J.C. PHILPOT · JAMES RENWICK · J.B. STONEY
HENRY TANNER · JOHN VINALL · JOHN WARBURTON
JOHN WELWOOD · GEORGE WHITEFIELD · J.A. WYLIE

Price £1.75 *(postage included)*
Issued Spring, Summer, Autumn, Winter.

Book Order Form

Please send to the address below:-

	Price	Quantity
A Question for Pope John Paul II	£1.25	......
Of God or Man?	£1.45	......
Noah and the Flood	£1.90	......
Divine Footsteps	£0.95	......
The Red Heifer	£0.75	......
The Wells of Salvation	£1.50	......
The Book of Ruth (Hardback edition)	£4.95	......
Divine Meditations of William Huntington	£2.35	......
Present-Day Conversions of the New Testament Kind	£2.25	......

Psalms, Hymns & Spiritual Songs (Hardback edition)

		Price	Quantity
The Psalms of the Old Testament		£2.50	......
Spiritual Songs from the Gospels		£2.50	......
The Hymns of the New Testament		£2.50	......

'Apostolic Foundation of the Christian Church' series

		Price	Quantity
Foundations Uncovered	Vol.I	£0.30	......
The Birth of Jesus Christ	Vol.II	£0.95	......
The Messiah	Vol.III	£2.45	......
The Son of God and Seed of David (Hardback edition)	Vol.IV	£6.95	......
Christ Crucified (Hardback edition)	Vol.V	£6.95	......
Justification by Faith (Hardback edition)	Vol.VI	£7.50	......
The Church: What is it? (Hardback edition)	Vol.VII	£7.75	......

Name and Address (in block capitals)

. . . .

. . . .

. . . .

If money is sent with order please allow for postage. Please address to:- The John Metcalfe Publishing Trust, Church Road, Tylers Green, Penn, Bucks, HP10 8LN.

cut here

xlix

Tract Order Form

Please send to the address below:-

		Price	Quantity
Evangelical Tracts			
The Two Prayers of Elijah		£0.10	......
Wounded for our Transgressions		£0.10	......
The Blood of Sprinkling		£0.10	......
The Grace of God that Brings Salvation		£0.10	......
The Name of Jesus		£0.10	......
The Ministry of the New Testament		£0.10	......
The Death of the Righteous by A.M.S.		£0.10	......
'Tract for the Times' series			
The Gospel of God	No.1	£0.25	......
The Strait Gate	No.2	£0.25	......
Eternal Sonship and Taylor Brethren	No.3	£0.25	......
Marks of the New Testament Church	No.4	£0.25	......
The Charismatic Delusion	No.5	£0.25	......
Premillennialism Exposed	No.6	£0.25	......
Justification and Peace	No.7	£0.25	......
Faith or presumption?	No.8	£0.25	......
The Elect undeceived	No.9	£0.25	......
Justifying Righteousness	No.10	£0.25	......
Righteousness Imputed	No.11	£0.25	......
The Great Deception	No.12	£0.25	......
A Famine in the Land	No.13	£0.25	......
Blood and Water	No.14	£0.25	......
Women Bishops?	No.15	£0.25	......
The Heavenly Vision	No.16	£0.25	......
Ecclesia Tracts			
The Beginning of the Ecclesia	No.1	£0.10	......
Churches and the Church (J.N.D.)	No.2	£0.10	......
The Ministers of Christ	No.3	£0.10	......
The Inward Witness (G.F.)	No.4	£0.10	......
The Notion of a Clergyman (J.N.D.)	No.5	£0.10	......
The Servant of the Lord (W.H.)	No.6	£0.10	......
One Spirit (W.K.)	No.7	£0.10	......
The Funeral of Arminianism (W.H.)	No.8	£0.10	......
One Body (W.K.)	No.9	£0.10	......
False Churches and True	No.10	£0.10	......
Separation from Evil (J.N.D.)	No.11	£0.10	......
The Remnant (J.B.S.)	No.12	£0.10	......

Name and Address (in block capitals)

. . . .

. . . .

. . . .

If money is sent with order please allow for postage. Please address to:- The
John Metcalfe Publishing Trust, Church Road, Tylers Green, Penn, Bucks, HP10 8LN.

cut here

Magazine Order Form

Name and Address (in block capitals)

. . . .

. . . .

. . . .

Please send me .... current copy/copies of The Ministry of the New Testament.

Please send me .... year/s subscription.

I enclose a cheque/postal order for £ ....

(Price: including postage, U.K. £1.75; Overseas £1.90)
(One year's subscription: Including postage, U.K. £7.00; Overseas £7.60)

Cheques should be made payable to The John Metcalfe Publishing Trust, and for overseas subscribers should be in pounds sterling drawn on a London Bank.

10 or more copies to one address will qualify for a 10% discount

Back numbers from Spring 1986 available.

Please send to The John Metcalfe Publishing Trust, Church Road, Tylers Green, Penn, Bucks, HP10 8LN

All Publications of the Trust are subsidised by the Publishers.